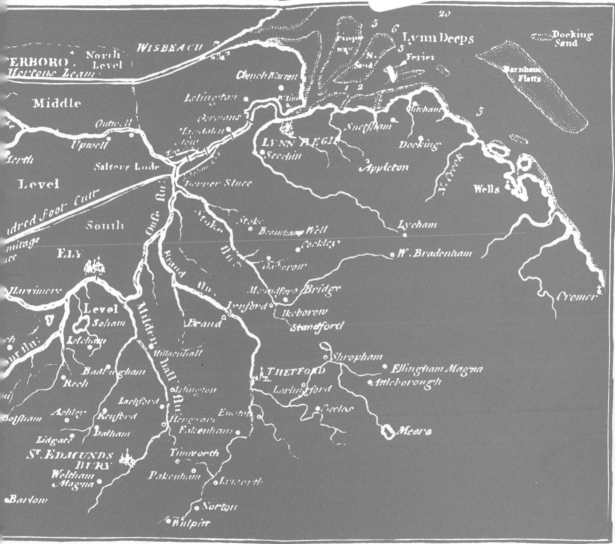

g head *in* NORTHAMPTON-SHI

LYNN *being about* 160 *Miles.*

FENLAND RIVER

To

Daddy,
lots of love,

Pauline xxx

Sept. 1975

FENLAND RIVER

The story of the Great Ouse and its Tributaries

by

RODNEY TIBBS

Foreword by W. E. Doran, Esq., O.B.E., B.A.I., M.I.C.E.
Chief Engineer, Great Ouse River Board, 1940 to 1962

TERENCE DALTON LIMITED
LAVENHAM · SUFFOLK
1969

Published by
TERENCE DALTON LIMITED
SBN 900963 10 7

Photo Engravings by
STAR ILLUSTRATION WORKS LIMITED

Printed in Great Britain at
THE LAVENHAM PRESS LIMITED
LAVENHAM   SUFFOLK

To Anna - Louise

The Publishers wish to thank all those who helped to provide illustrations for this book. Many local newspapers gave valuable assistance at short notice and are to be congratulated on the very high standard of their photographic skills.

PHOTOGRAPHS, also acknowledged in text, were provided by The Bedfordshire Times; The Bury Free Press; Cambridge News; Ely Standard; Forestry Commission; Lynn News and Advertiser; Michael Manni; D. Monk; Norwich Union Insurance Group; Studio Five, Thetford, and Rodney Tibbs who also provided the colour picture for the dust jacket. MAPS. Endpapers and those on pages 91 and 93 by kind permission of Cambridge University Library. Chapter Head maps and diagrammatic map in Appendix Two are by Graham Mugliston.

The chapter head maps are based upon the Ordnance Survey map with the sanction of the Controller of H.M. Stationery Office. Crown Copyright reserved. Each is marked "Crown Copyright".

CONTENTS

INDEX OF ILLUSTRATIONS

The Author, Rodney Tibbs, at work aboard a cruiser on the Ouse

M. Manni

ACKNOWLEDGEMENT

MANY books have briefly referred to the river Great Ouse, but only a few have approached it in greater detail. Fewer still have started where the Ouse starts, in Northamptonshire and followed it through to the Wash in Norfolk and it is only after one has attempted a book on the Great Ouse that this diffidence on the part of its chroniclers becomes clear. The fascinating waterways of which this river is the key are so over-rich in detail, history and surprise that the task of taking an overall look becomes particularly daunting.

I can only justify my approach by urging the reader to regard this volume as an informative companion for anyone fortunate enough to cruise its waters, relax on its green and rushy banks or simply to engage in the pursuit of greater knowledge of its present and past.

Fenmen and others who have this great waterway close to their hearts are, in my experience, ever ready to answer the questions of those whose interest brings them under its spell. Many helped in the preparation of this book. Some offered advice from its banks, others propped up a handy gate or downed a pint as they recalled bygone days or organised the future. One would like to thank them all even though a number, with Fenland modesty, departed without offering a name.

The experts have played their part as well. Mr. W. K. Masters, Chief Engineer of the Great Ouse River Authority and Mr. C. H. Fennell the Authority's Fisheries Officer willingly offered specialised knowledge and advice. I am indebted to Mr. W. C. Fincham, better known as "The Fenman" of the "Cambridge News", whose knowledge of angling in Ouse waters is encyclopaedic and based on a lifetime's familiarity with the Fens. Appreciation must also be expressed to the management of Cambridge Newspapers Ltd. for permission to use various photographs and material, and to the secretary and staff of the Cambridge University Library for their expert advice and assistance and for permission to use the illustrations on pages 91, 93 and end papers.

Of the many others who brought special skills to the book I would thank Graham Mugliston for his work on the chapter title maps, John Venmore-Rowland from my publishers for advice and helpfulness in the preparation of the manuscript far exceeding the normal bounds of duty, Mr. W. E. Doran, former Chief Engineer of the Great Ouse River Board for much valuable information and guidance and Michael Manni who dared to venture on the waterways with me and brought home some excellent photographs.

Rodney Tibbs

FOREWORD

by

W. E. DORAN Esq., o.b.e., b.a.i., m.i.c.e.

Chief Engineer, Great Ouse River Board, 1940 to 1962.

A FTER a very pleasant dinner some years ago in one of the Cambridge Colleges a certain Don turned to me and said "Why is the Ouse like a flea?". I was unable to think of any reasonable answer to this conundrum. "Ha!" he said "eighteenth century that one, because it goes into Beds. and Hunts. and ends up in the Wash!" I suspect that he made it up himself!

The Author of this book, Rodney Tibbs, has not been guilty of making anything up himself but he has succeeded in making our journey along the Ouse and its tributaries most interesting and agreeable without turning it into just another guide book. No easy task!

I have been associated with the Ouse area for twenty seven years. One of my first tasks, on joining the Great Ouse Catchment Board, as it was in 1936, was to proceed with plans for the restoration of the derelict navigation.

The reader will find an account of the affray between the Ashleys and the Jemmatts in the 17th century but this was not the last of the battles to be fought over the Ouse navigation.

In the 1890s the navigation had fallen into decay. The story goes that it was put up for auction by the widow of the then proprietor. There were few bidders but it was bought by a Mr. Simpson. He was reported to have said later that he would not have done it if he hadn't had so good a lunch! However that may be, having bought it, he set about manfully to put it in order up to Bedford. The cost was considerable but in a few years the task was nearly complete.

In 1894 there came a very high flood. Godmanchester was in peril from the rapidly rising flood waters. To help to relieve the threat the Mayor ordered the lock gates to be forced open. This was resisted by Simpson and his employees. The Mayor and Corporation quoted their Charter giving them the right to have the gates open—and open them they did.

The sequel was an action in the High Court, Simpson v Godmanchester. The Judge ruled that their Charter from King John gave the men of Godmanchester the right to open the lock gates in time of danger. This was a bitter blow for Simpson after all his expense and hard work. He was so incensed that he gave orders to sink barges in front of the lock gates and the gates to be padlocked or secured with iron straps. Simpson was right in thinking that his locks could be seriously damaged by being used

for flood water discharge. The men of Godmanchester were right in thinking that opening the lock gates would help to let the flood water get away. So ended, after a very brief revival, the commercial navigation on the River Ouse.

Meanwhile the deterioration of the fenland flood banks and river channels and periodic flooding of lands along the Bedford Ouse were causing serious concern. A Royal Commission was set up in 1927 and its recommendations resulted finally in the 1930 Land Drainage Act under which Catchment Boards were set up to deal with the drainage and flood problems of the principal rivers of England and Wales.

The Great Ouse Catchment Board commenced operations in 1932. It found itself faced with the task of repairing and raising over 100 miles of flood banks in the Fens, the dredging of silted up rivers and, in the upper reaches of the rivers, the reconstruction of derelict sluices and weirs.

Its predecessor, The Great Ouse Drainage Board, had made a start on the most urgent work but was hampered by an almost complete lack of funds and an unworkable rating system. So far as the main River Ouse was concerned the free passage of floods was prevented by numerous mills and inadequate sluices. Simpson's derelict navigation was purchased. Steel sluices had already been installed at Brownshill, St. Ives, Houghton, Hemingford and Huntingdon by the Ouse Drainage Board but still the capacity was inadequate. The first thing to do was to use the locks for extra discharge capacity.

The timber "pointing doors" of locks cannot be used for discharge regulation and the locks themselves would be undermined by such use. This is the reason for the steel lifting gates in the locks which are not popular with boat users! In addition lock floors had to be lowered and work done at the downstream end to safeguard the structures from damage from the high velocity of flow. The programme was interrupted by the war but the Ouse is now navigable to Tempsford. To continue up to Bedford would be a very costly operation and there seems to be little prospect, under present circumstances, of it being done.

There is certainly a great attraction in the idea of a quiet and peaceful holiday in the idyllic surroundings of a gently flowing stream. Herein lies the seed of self destruction. The throttle happy gentleman in the motor cruiser who swishes past the fishermen at full speed and the ubiquitous transistor sets screaming out the latest pop records are an increasing menace.

However the Ouse river system is large and far flung and it is still possible to escape from one's fellow man. Perhaps, dear reader, you should try it before it is too late!

Haslemere,
Surrey.
October, 1968.

Chapter One

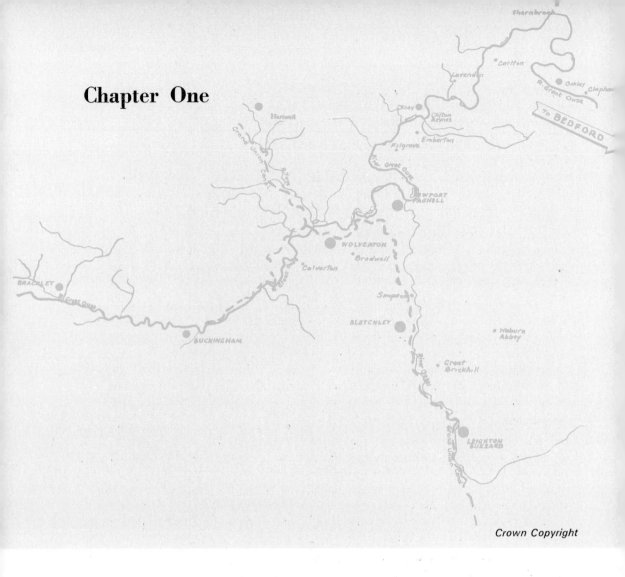

ONE freezing December day I found myself in the front cockpit of a Tiger Moth biplane—one of those early machines that have changed little since the day they were designed, over 30 years ago. There were few refinements and certainly no comfortable closed cockpit to protect the two occupants from the weather. A small windscreen did its best to shield me from the blast of the propeller and a simple rubber speaking tube provided communication with the pilot at the rear.

It was in 1965 and we were off to have a look at the Great Ouse which, as the result of heavy rainfall, had risen to the point at which the land forming part of the river flood plains and washes had been submerged. We climbed slowly through damp clear air above Cambridge. From three thousand feet the spires of King's College chapel looked like the miniature battlements on a Victorian wedding cake and the surrounding colleges like so many pieces of decoration in white icing. The large compass pointed north east and peering through the wing struts I could locate Grafham Water lying alongside the Great Ouse in Bedfordshire. But that was not our destination since Grafham is not of the winter but of a warm breezy summer's day, of sailing dinghies, cucumber sandwiches and iced lager.

Below us was the Huntingdon Road which we followed to St. Ives. At Longstanton the floods began and field after field was under water—water that was strangely clear, so much so that the furrows and tufts of grass were clearly visible from the air.

It is not unusual for the Ouse to be in flood at this time of the year and the scene below us was not as alarming as it might possibly have appeared to a stranger. The river might have lost its outline in the flooded fields but in most cases this was exactly what it was intended it should do. Large areas on either side of the river from St. Ives outwards through the Fens are set aside as 'wash land'. It is over these predetermined areas, contained within hundreds of miles of earth banking, that any excess flow from Bedfordshire and Buckinghamshire is allowed to spread harmlessly.

We circled St. Ives, the arches of its famous bridge were only just clear of the rushing torrent. Motor cruisers at the quayside rode at their moorings and the occasional tiny figure looked up at the yellow and silver biplane as we passed overhead. In seconds we had accomplished the run upstream to Holywell which, in a boat, has taken me several pleasant and leisurely hours. The Ferry Boat Inn, reputed to be the oldest in Britain, had the water up to its front door and I knew that the villagers would be taking the top path for their pint that night. Slowly we lost height and passed over the picturesque thatched pub with the engine popping and spluttering at the idle. Someone came out, looked up and waved—a tiny spirited figure of a man undaunted by the acre upon acre of water we saw washing his village.

At Earith we flew ruler straight to the north, our path picked out on the left by the Old Bedford River and on the right, a hundred yards or so away, by the New Bedford River or Hundred Foot Drain. We gazed down in wonder at these titanic cuts made across the face of the Fens under the skilled direction of Sir Cornelius Vermuyden, the Dutch engineer and genius in the grand manner, as part of his drainage scheme which produced some of the richest farming land in the world.

Soon we peeled off to the right, looked at Ely sitting on the original course of the Ouse, and returned along the river as it snaked its way to Cambridge and our home airfield. We had seen a cold, grey Ouse whipped into myriads of tiny wavelets by the icy winds of the Fens. But of all the rivers the Ouse possesses an immense and basic character. It begins miles away in Northamptonshire, skirts a mile or so of the Oxford border and then passes through Buckinghamshire, Bedfordshire, Huntingdonshire and thence Cambridgeshire and the Isle of Ely into Norfolk to enter the Wash at Kings Lynn. A river whose tributaries add Suffolk, Hertfordshire and Essex to the impressive list of counties in which it flows.

Its name, the Great Ouse, is by no means the jolliest of titles for a river. To the stranger it may suggest sluggish murky depths, a forbidding waterway, a styx wending its way through a desolate landscape. Not so. It is true that the Ouse—Fenmen always omit the 'Great'— never hurries. Like the men of Upware, Earith, Denver and beyond it takes life as it comes and refuses to be hurried. Even as a tiny stream in Northampton-shire and Buckinghamshire it moves with an unhurried pace. Some rivers are simply pretty, others a happy gurgle but the Ouse is a fully adult waterway and one of the major rivers of Great Britain. It can swop pleasant views with the best of them as it winds its way between Huntingdon and St. Ives and it is on nodding terms with the commercial waterways as it runs side by side with the Grand Union Canal between Buckingham and Stony Stratford.

It is a river of relaxation, of splendid boating and magnificent fishing but it is also a life and death waterway and one which carries the full responsibility for making hundreds of square miles habitable by man. Few rivers in this country make such a vital contribution to the countryside through which they flow as the Ouse does as it passes through Earith before making its devious way to the sea.

But its youth is spent in the gentle countryside of Buckinghamshire. Anyone pottering in this area has much to see and the river is by far the best place from which to explore. The pleasures of this county are small but perfect, shy but well worth seeking out. Stowe is the exception. There is nothing miniature about Stowe and the river, as if surprised by the grandeur of this eighteenth century mansion, makes a wide, semi-circular detour around it to the south. It eyes the building warily as if aware that it is unlikely to meet anything quite so grand in the rest of its travels. Stowe is best known today as a famous public school but it is equally important as an example of English architecture and landscape design. It is connected to the river at Buckingham by a superb three mile avenue of beech trees.

The house itself is about a quarter of a mile long while the parkland covers about 800 acres. In wandering around the grounds (the only part open to the public and then only at Easter weekend and for a fortnight in August) the visitor cannot fail to be impressed by their layout which was the work of William Kent, Capability Brown and others. It is of interest to note that the church in the grounds is the only thing that remains of an entire village which was destroyed when the house was built, and the grounds were laid out in 1713. The church provides another surprise for the observant. An altar tomb carries a number of charming portraits including one of a small Eliza-bethan boy dressed in Tudor costume as if he were grown up. A brass inscription announces that he was born on 31st October 1592 and died on 1st January 1592. The inscription is correct for at that time New Year's Day was in March! Stowe is rich in

Stowe House

R. Tibbs

garden ornaments and building but, like most good things in Buckinghamshire, it is necessary to seek them out. Peter Scheemakers was commissioned to produce many of the statues but this work he shared with Rysbrack. The gardens are important as an object lesson in visual planning. Some of our modern planners and designers could learn much from a visit—they might even get to grips with the true conception of a vista. The main approach first reveals and then conceals the house. It gives fascinating glimpses of what Brown called the Elysian Fields and the lake then turns sharply into the long vista, between the Boycott Pavilions, before ending in the north forecourt of the house.

Buckingham, which is embraced on three sides by the Ouse, is rich in old buildings and provides some superb views over and beyond the river. On top of the clock tower is a swan, the county emblem, a reminder that Buckingham was the county town until superseded by Aylesbury. In the market place is a castle shaped building which once

The Church at Stowe—all that remains of the village   *R. Tibbs*

served as a gaol. At one time Buckingham was an important wool trading centre of which the river and nearby canal played an important part. When exploring the river here you will probably come across the site of a church which now lies in crumbled ruins. The tombs are covered with a green mantle of ivy and an occasional cherub still manages to smile from the eroded stone from which it was carved. Flowers grow wild in the shade of pines and cypresses and around the stump of a cross that is slowly mouldering away.

A short distance downstream the Ouse is joined by the River Tove just above Wolverton and a little further down by the River Ousel which had its beginning near

The lake at Stowe

A quiet corner of Buckingham   R. *Tibbs*

Leighton Buzzard. These silent waterways, popular with anglers and excellent haunts for the owner of a private boat especially if he inclines towards ornithology—or for that matter any other 'ology' indicating an interest in nature.

Olney lies right on the course of the Ouse and was, for nineteen years, the home of William Cowper. It was here that he wrote most of his poems and hymns. Many, however, will know of Olney for its very famous Shrove Tuesday pancake race of which the first was reputed to have been run in 1445. In 1950 the town received and accepted a challenge from the town of Liberal, in the State of Kansas, U.S.A. This has now become an annual Anglo-American event which sticks to the time-honoured rules—only women can compete over the quarter mile course and the pancakes have to be tossed at least three times during the run.

At Wolverton the Ouse is surrounded by pleasant meadows whilst the town dreams nostalgically of its long and important connection with railways. It was here

The Great Ouse near Buckingham   R. *Tibbs*

that the old London, Midland and Scottish Railway Company built its great works and set up a centre to teach, in the early days, rail traffic control. This was at a time when men stood on the tracks and gave signals not unlike those of a traffic warden or policeman of to-day. There were an unusual number of signal posts near Wolverton station and thus it was an ideal spot for giving the trainees practice. They were taught to stand erect to signal that the line was clear, to wave a red flag if it were not or there was other danger and to bring the flag smartly to the shoulder, as if in salute, when the engine passed. Things have changed a little since then.

At Newport Pagnell, well known for the traffic jams when there is motor racing on the Silverstone circuit, a fine stone bridge of five arches allows the Ouse to flow under the A.50. It is near this town that the river is joined by the River Lovat. On the banks of the Ouse and close to the church, Tickford Abbey preserves the name of a priory founded in the days of William Rufus. The present house contains some relics of the old building, stones with Norman carving in the garden wall, and a piece of old glass in the kitchen showing a man, an angel and a sleeping woman. Make of that what you will since I can offer no explanation.

This chapter began with memories of flying over the Ouse. I have bitter memories of flying over Newport Pagnell in an aircraft owned by the Automobile Association. The M.1. motorway, of which the original stretch formed a bypass to the town, was still under construction. It was a perfect day on the ground with small puffy white cumulus clouds dotting a clear blue sky. In the air it meant bumpy conditions and for me, airsickness. I can remember little of the countryside of the journey apart from the fact that I longed for something dramatic to happen to put me out of my misery—it didn't and I had to be content to sit patiently, if not silently, to await our landing.

From Newport Pagnell the Ouse makes its way towards Bedford but it seems in little hurry to get there. It wanders by the splendid camping site at Chellington Pavenham and on to provide an excellent stretch of water for sailing at Oakley. This is a very pleasant little village just outside Bedford which spills gracefully over a small valley at the foot of some hills. It has Jacobean farmhouses and cottages nestling in the trees. A fourteenth century tower with a small spire graces the church which still has much fine Norman work. Certainly not Norman but extremely fascinating is the barrel organ which was used to accompany the singing of the choir in the eighteenth century. There is also a long peephole arranged to allow fourteenth century Lords of the Manor to see, from their transcept, the altar in the new chancel.

Oakley also houses Bedfordshire's only pack of foxhounds although neighbouring packs the Fitzwilliam, the Whaddon Chase, the Pytchley and the Cambridgeshire often hunt within the county. The Hon. George Charles Granley Fitzharding Berkeley, the youngest son of the Fifth Earl of Berkeley is a famous figure from Oakley's past. He took over the hunt kennels and established himself at Harrold Hall: a real character if ever there was one, he once fought a duel with the editor of a magazine because it contained unfavourable comments on his novel "Berkeley Castle" and he learned pugilism from Jackson, the man who taught Byron. His book "Reminiscences of a Huntsman" is a jolly work which contains some excellent descriptions of the countryside around the river which he knew so well.

The county emblem, a swan, on Buckingham Town Hall

R. Tibbs

The old gaol at Buckingham is now an unusual cafe

R. Tibbs

Chapter Two

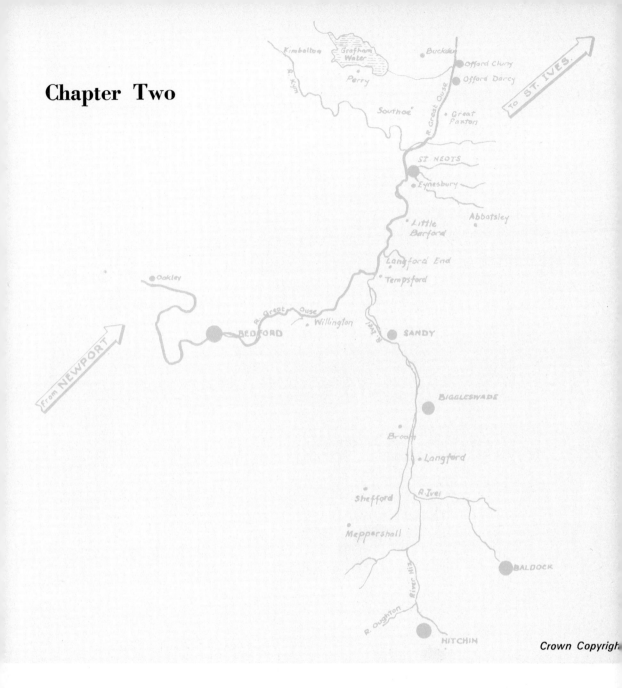

B Y the time it reaches Bedford the Ouse is a fully adult river. The town and water complement one another and the wide stream, well suited to boating and rowing, flows slowly between excellent river walks and graceful bridges and gardens. The catchment area of the Ouse makes a big impression upon the entire county, a factor which is not really surprising when one considers that the river crosses the length of Bedfordshire, a county that is rarely more than 20 miles wide. In this relatively short section the Ouse is joined by a number of small rivers including the Ivel and the Hiz.

The Ivel runs into the Ouse at Tempsford and it is this river and the gravel beds associated with it which make such a large contribution to the richness of the market garden soil in the Biggleswade region. Both as it approaches and leaves Bedford the Ouse valley exhibits all the characteristics of the truly English river scene. Here are the broad rich lush meadows full of unhurried cattle, dotted with alder and willow trees and punctuated with the occasional church spire or tower.

One of the best known names associated with Bedford is that of John Bunyan. Born at nearby Elstow in 1628 Bunyan enlisted in Cromwell's Parliamentary Army at 16 years of age at Newport Pagnell—a career in which he appears to have failed to distinguish himself. He established a reputation as a Nonconformist preacher for which he was persecuted and finally indicted, on the score "that he devilishly and perniciously abstained from coming to church to hear Divine Service . . . " Whilst the majority of his 12 year sentence was spent in the County Gaol he was, for a time, incarcerated in a small prison built on the bridge that crossed the Ouse at Bedford. There, it is claimed, he wrote part of his famous "Pilgrim's Progress" The bridge was later replaced by the existing splendid five arch one designed by Wing.

A small museum at the Bunyan Meeting House today contains a number of interesting mementos of this Bedfordshire preacher whose statue stands at the northern end of Bedford's High Street.

There is much of historical value at Bedford. Particularly interesting are some of the exhibits at the Prichard Memorial Museum which, in addition to the more usual antiquities, also houses some airship relics. There is the camera lens from the R.101, the compass stand of the R.100 and the cooking pots of the R.34. Both the R.100 and the R.34 made crossings of the Atlantic, the former completing the flight in 72 hours from Cardington just outside Bedford. It was from this same station that the R.101 took off on its last fateful flight which was to end in disaster on a hillside at Beauvais in France. The great airship hangars in which it was built are still at Cardington, gigantic memorials to a bygone era. Today this RAF station plays a similar role but with lighter than air balloons rather than the rigid airships.

I always feel that the Ouse becomes a rather placid and un-exciting river after it has left Bedford to flow gently onwards towards Great Barford, St. Neots, Huntingdon and Godmanchester. But if things are quiet and peaceful today it has not always been so.

In the seventeenth century the Ouse formed the nucleus of a number of navigable rivers and earned the description "a goodly fair river" when it was surveyed by Sir Clement Edmondes in 1618. But in the Great Barford, St. Neots area it was found to be "generally foul and overgrown with weeds" and "stopped with weirs" between Huntingdon and Ely. Sir Clement was primarily concerned with the river as a channel for fen drainage but the records show that it was also important from the point of view of navigation. In 1617 John Gason of Finchley secured certain rights on the Ouse which gave him power to make the river navigable where necessary for a period of 21 years. He assigned his rights over the rivers of Bedfordshire, Huntingdonshire and Cambridgeshire to Arnold Spencer and to Thomas Girton, a vintner of Westminster.

Spencer and Girton lost no time in getting busy and built six sluices between St. Ives and St. Neots, at Hemingford, Houghton, Godmanchester, Brampton, Offord and St. Neots designed to assist the passage of boats. The stretch from St. Ives to Great Barford was made navigable although in later years it was allowed to fall into disrepair. Toll rights on the river seem to have been profitable in those days: and these rights were transferred by Spencer and Girton to a number of people.

The market at Bedford *Bedfordshire Times*

In due course the Jemmatt and the Ashley families gained control over large sections of this part of the river and there were many quarrels over the rights to tolls. On 9th September, 1697, the Jemmatts stopped a group of lighters near Great Barford and refused to allow them to continue up the river to Bedford. An ugly scene developed when Henry Ashley junior ordered the watermen to "set down" or lower Great Barford staunch so that the boats could continue on their journey. Charles Wood, an employee of the Jemmatts, "endeavoured to displace some of the boards as they were setting" by using the end of his cane. One of the watermen "gave the said Mr. Wood ill language" and challenged him to a fight. Order was not restored until the constable of Great Barford finally arrived to sort things out. But the story does not end there. The next morning at eight o'clock, Ashley, who was also a Justice of the Peace and had evidently decided to overlook his duties in that direction, arrived at The Bull in Great Barford where Wood was lodging. He had with him two swords and challenged Wood to a duel, but Wood, showing rather more commonsense than the magistrate, declined the offer. The scene then shifted to the Court of Chancery where a decision was made in Ashley's favour. Even so he did not get the money owed to him until many years later when £150. 16. 3d. was handed over by the son of John and Ann Jemmatt, the originators of the trouble.

From the somewhat colourful goings on in the 17th century we are reminded of a more modern piece of Great Ouse history—the building of Grafham Water, a reservoir which is the largest area of man-made water in the country. But it is not just a reservoir but an imaginative development bringing pleasure and excellent facilities to anglers, boating and sailing enthusiasts, naturalists and many others.

The first stage of the scheme, begun in 1963 and opened by the Duke of Edinburgh on 6th July 1966, provided a reservoir covering 1,700 acres, holding 13,000 million gallons of water and just over three miles long by one and a half miles wide. Grafham Water draws its water from the Ouse at Offord by means of a sector gate which maintains the river at its correct level. Treated water in bulk from this £12,000,000 project is supplied to six public water undertakings serving an area of 1,960 square miles and a population of 1.4 million people. A second stage of the scheme will enable even larger quantities of water to be supplied.

In the early days of the scheme it was called Diddington Reservoir. Later the name was changed when it was realised that an error in map reading had been made and that it would be much nearer to Grafham.

There was a tremendous outcry from the farmers in the region when the great concrete wall, which is such a dramatic feature of the scheme, first began to appear on the landscape. They fought a brave but losing battle against the scheme and eventually seven farms and 20 houses were swallowed up as the reservoir was filled. Even those who designed and built the scheme watched sadly as the chimney pots of houses, which had once housed families and knew the laughter of children, disappeared for

Sailing at Grafham Water   R. Tibbs

good beneath the rising flood. But in their place have come many activities which make the stretch of the Ouse between Bedford and Huntingdon particularly attractive to a wide range of people.

The Grafham Water Sailing Club is probably the most active local organisation and the Huntingdonshire and Peterborough County Councils contributed £100,000 toward the cost of sailing facilities. As a result the club has a splendid clubhouse and other buildings as well as a number of slipways. In this ideal setting for competitive racing many and varied class boats such as Ospreys, Flying 15s, Fireballs, Enterprises, 12 ft. Nationals and G.P. 14s can be seen heeling to the breeze and skimming gracefully across the water under a summer's sky. Club membership quickly reached the 1,500 mark with enthusiasts who came from as far away as Coventry, Stamford and London.

Grafham Water, which was originally stocked with 68,000 trout, has been described as "the best trout fishing ground in Europe" and therefore is of considerable interest to anglers. Over 10,000 trout were caught during the 1966 season and on a single day that year 400 anglers fished the lake. The Great Ouse Water Authority have spent a considerable sum on stocking the reservoir with fish—in one season alone they spent £8,000 and a further £2,350 to improve the original stock of trout.

The cost of fishing at Grafham may vary from season to season but the average is about £1 a day for an adult fishing from the bank and about seven shillings and sixpence for a child who must be accompanied by a permit holder. A season ticket costs around £40 whilst powered fishing boats can be hired for about £5 a day and rowing boats for about £2—part day hire is also possible.

Naturalists soon found that the presence of such a large area of water created a splendid environment for many birds and wildfowl. In fact the water sprang a surprise of its own quite early on when complaints began to come in from nearby residents who were invaded by large clouds of mosquitoes. This particular nuisance now seems to have disappeared but there remains a wealth of flora and fauna for fruitful study.

The Bedfordshire and Huntingdonshire Naturalists Trust has now set up a nature reserve at Grafham which covers 200 acres and about two miles of the reservoir bank. They man the area with volunteer wardens and have provided a splendid hide from which ducks, moorhens and wildfowl can be watched with pleasure and in comfort. Two floating islands have also been set up. A luxury village, aimed at providing even better facilities for those who visit the area to enjoy the amenities, was planned at nearby Perry.

Anyone exploring this section of waterway around Grafham will find the further tributaries of the Ouse worthy of investigation. The River Ivel reaches the Ouse at Tempsford having set out across country from the Baldock, Stevenage direction. It passes close by the pretty Cambridgeshire village of Ashwell, from which the famous Ashwell Springs provide the initial outfall for the beginnings of another famous

Club house of the Grafham Water Sailing Club

R. Tibbs

tributary of the Ouse, the Rhee which runs into the Cam on its way to the University City of Cambridge and "The Backs".

The Ivel is joined in turn by a river with an odd name indeed, the Hiz, into which the Rivers Oughton and Purwell come from the Hitchin area. It was at Tempsford that the Danes threw up a small square series of defensive earthworks still to be seen in the south west of the village and known as the Gannocks. Here the Danes took refuge when they left their headquarters at Huntingdon and moved up the Ouse to its junction with the Ivel. Quantities of palaeolithic stone implements of the more primitive kind have been found at this spot to provide evidence that man had inhabited the place for many thousands of years. At Eaton Socon, not far from Tempsford, a mammoth carcass was discovered; a reminder of the Ice Age.

Further north are other interesting tributaries. The River Til provides some delightful scenes and vistas as it makes its way up from Rushden to become the River Kym near the grounds of Kimbolton Castle. It is the Kym, winding happily along south of Grafham Water, which brings us back to St. Neots.

The bridge and river, Bedford, at Regatta time *Bedfordshire Times*

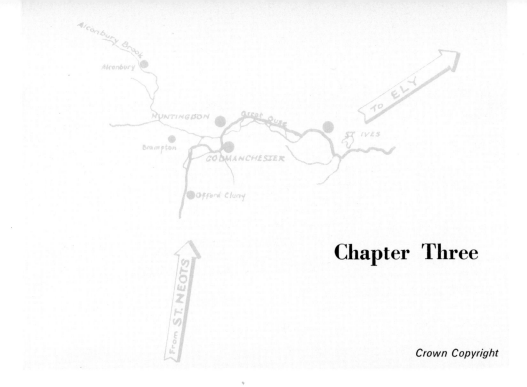

Chapter Three

APART from writing "Robinson Crusoe", Daniel Defoe travelled and wrote extensively about the British Isles. In his "Tour Through the Whole Island of Gt. Britain" he made an observation which I must admit had never occurred to me before.

"Another thing is scarce to be equallid in the whole isle of Britain; namely, that tho' the Ouse, by a long and winding course, cuts through the county (*Bedfordshire*), and by its long reachings, so as to make above seventy miles between Oulney and St. Neots, tho' not above twenty by land, yet in all that course it receives but one river into it, namely the little River Ivel, which falls into the Ouse a little above Tempesford." Even today Defoe remains basically correct.

Not many years back St. Neots formed one of the worst road bottlenecks on the A.45 running from Cambridge across to the A.1. This hold-up was caused by a splendid bridge built in the fourteenth century to which walls were added in the seventeenth century. Recently the old bridge was removed, in spite of protestation from local residents, and a fine new road bridge was built across the Ouse at this point. Saint Neot himself was a monk of Glastonbury and had the reputation "of being humble to all, affable in conversation, wise in transacting business, venerable in aspect, severe in countenance, moderate even in his walk, sincere, upright, calm temperate and charitable." Had he been alive at the time I often wonder if this paragon would have let his hair down a bit the day they took away the equally venerable bridge of St. Neots, the market town named after him?

There is good boating, sailing and fishing here and anyone with the time and the inclination can spend a pleasant hour or so cruising down the river to the county town of Huntingdon. I make no apology for returning to Defoe for he put the point very well. "Here are the most beautiful meadows on the banks of the River Ouse, that I think are to be seen in any part of England; and to see them in the summer season, cover'd with such innumerable stocks of cattle and sheep, is one of the most agreeable sights of its kind in the world".

Defoe found the town of Huntingdon unremarkable but here I think he was being a little uncharitable. Perhaps, however, I am being prejudiced since to me the town marks the beginning of one of the most beautiful stretches of the Ouse as it meanders from Huntingdon through the Hemingfords to St. Ives. It is as if the river is conscious of the fact that it is about to meet the totally different mood and austere

The new road bridge at St. Neots   *Cambridge News*

The old road and new pedestrian bridges at Huntingdon *Cambridge News*

setting of the Fens and puts on a last, inspired show of splendour. Huntingdon retains what St. Neots has lost—a fine ancient bridge which, although a curse to modern traffic, is a delight to the eye. Until recently pedestrians had to live dangerously to cross the bridge but now, but a few feet away, is an elegant modern foot bridge.

Just outside Huntingdon, at Godmanchester, the ancient Roman bridgehead on the Ouse, the river forms two loops. One of these flows under the famous "willow pattern" bridge near which stands the quaint little Town Hall where Godmanchester's Mayor and Corporation have deliberated for many centuries. Joining Huntingdon to Godmanchester is a fine raised causeway. Originally constructed about 1300 this was rebuilt in 1637 by Robert Cooke who narrowly escaped drowning while crossing the low meadows when the river was in flood. Two bridges which were built into this causeway allow flood waters to run through.

Huntingdon is perhaps best known as the birth place, in 1599, of Oliver Cromwell.

The Chinese "willow pattern" bridge, Godmanchester *R. Tibbs*

The house where he was born and the school building in which he was educated still remain. Whilst it is not possible to visit the house it is possible to see over the garden. Samuel Pepys was educated at the same school and nearby Brampton is but one of the many places claiming to be where the redoubtable Samuel first saw the light of day— so many make this claim that they must surely rival the number of beds in which England's Virgin Queen is claimed to have slept. The school building now houses the Cromwell museum and contains numerous Cromwellian relics. At Brampton Pepys' house can be seen, by special arrangement with the owner, and remember to take a good look at the garden for it was here that the Diarist is said to have buried his money when he feared a Dutch invasion.

The poet Cowper, who was also born at Huntingdon, was obviously biased towards the town if one compares the slightly disparaging remarks of Defoe with his own remarks about the place. Cowper wrote "The longer I live here the better I like the place and the people who belong to it. I am on very good terms with no less than four families, beside two or three old scrambling fellows like myself." Of the Ouse he wrote "It is the most agreeable circumstance in this part of the world. A noble stream to bathe in, and I shall make use of it three times a week having introduced myself to it first this morning."

Quaint boathouses at Godmanchester

R. Tibbs

A riverside scene reflected in the Ouse at Godmanchester

R. Tibbs

Cowper however was not plagued by one thing that assails the ears of local residents today. Huntingdon is ringed by a number of English and American Air Force stations, from which the sound of jet engines add their own disturbing din. To the north west is the huge American installation at Alconbury, which acts as a surplus equipment disposal centre for the whole of the U.S. Air Force in Europe. Here dealers bid for anything from thimbles to surplus aircraft. Members of the public who call at the American surplus equipment shop, at nearby Molesworth, can find a staggering range of items. I have seen such things as washing machines and refrigerators sold at very low prices and it is quite easy to discover some real bargains among the large number of books available at the shop. I have been offered a tractor and a lawn mower and I have seen babies' cots standing alongside enormous fish and chip frying ranges.

To the north of Huntingdon is R.A.F. Upwood, famous as a bomber base during World War II while to the east is Wyton, an R.A.F. base which pioneered photo reconnaisance and from which giant "V" bombers can be seen heaving themselves into the sky.

Like St. Neots, Huntingdon has taken part in the Greater London Overspill Scheme, a method by which the Greater London and local Councils co-operate to provide new housing estates and factories designed to attract Londoners and industry into the area. Huntingdon is the richer for the new and thriving industries that have been established and the London families have settled, on the whole, remarkably well into their new green and picturesque country environment.

Just down the road is Kimbolton Castle upon which Catherine of Aragon once gazed with the air of a woman who had learned bitter lessons from the past. She was banished from the court of Henry VIII and, in failing health, lived at Kimbolton for three years until her death. During the early part of her banishment she stayed at Buckden Palace near Kimbolton, the home of the Bishop of Lincoln whose diocese at that time stretched from the Humber to the Thames. Not much of the palace remains today, but there is a fine tower and gatehouse in red brick, probably dating from 1490; the grounds can be visited during parts of August and September. Kimbolton Castle is now a school, and can also be visited at certain times of the year.

After Hartford and Wyton the Ouse flows on to three magnificent examples of the English countryside at its best, Houghton, Hemingford Abbots and Hemingford Grey. All are delightful and near perfect examples of old building and superb river scenery. Potto Brown lived at Houghton, a rich miller and a non-conformist who believed that there were few things more efficaceous in times of difficulty than a little prayer. He accordingly took his ledgers with him to church and told God who owed him money—and their names! He always refused to be photographed and when he died there was nothing to remember him by except a small pencil silhouette sketch of him. A nearby farmer named Albert Goodman who had never done anything at all artistic in his life shut himself away for several days with a suitable lump of plaster. He produced an excellent bust which has since been cast in bronze and now stands in the village for all to see.

Both Hemingford Grey and Houghton have beautiful old water mills in delightful settings and it is interesting to note that the Domesday Book records earlier mills in both villages. The manor of Hemingford had "a mill worth annually ten shillings" while the Manor of Houghton had "one mill worth annually twenty shillings". There

Boats at Houghton

R. Tibbs

River scene near the Hemingfords

R. Tibbs

is doubt among scholars as to whether windmills were in use during the early years of the Norman Conquest. However the Domesday Book refers to a number of mills for which there was not an obvious supply of water and this tends to support the argument that windmills were known.

Houghton Mill is a particularly fine example which eked out the last of its active life by breaking up cattle cake. When redundant it was originally bought by the villagers in order that it might be preserved and it is now a Youth Hostel.

The Ouse wanders on through still, deep pools broken in the evenings by the fish rising to the surface, and leaping upwards to catch the dancing gnats and other insects as they skim above the stream.

Not far away the famous Huntingdonshire town of St. Ives spans the river. To approach by river is to get the best possible view of the magnificent old bridge which, even today, is the sole means of access to the town for all traffic from the south. The bridge was of wood until 1384 and in 1645 had its southern arch turned into a drawbridge. Today it is one of two such bridges in the country which have a small chapel perched in the centre. The other is at Wakefield and the chapel differs a little from the St. Ives version which some time ago had its upper storey removed—it was in good company for in World War I the local church spire was struck and knocked down by an aeroplane. Twice before this the spire had come down, once it simply succumbed to old age and on another occasion it was struck by lightning.

Towards the western end of St. Ives is an excellent quay alongside which boats can be moored. The town indeed makes an excellent base for anyone cruising on this section of the river. To have moored at St. Ives on a placid summer evening or a bright spring morning with the smell of cooking drifting from the galley is to have experienced something quite unforgettable.

A barn, alleged to have been owned by Cromwell, was one of the sights of St. Ives but in recent years, and in spite of much protest, it was pulled down. But Cromwell's statue still dominates the little market place and makes an excellent starting point from which to explore on foot the many little side streets and alleyways which abound in this quaint little town. The name St. Ives is derived from St. Ivo, a somewhat elusive Saint, who is said to have come from Persia in the seventh century. At that time the town was known as Slepe and it was here that St. Ivo was buried. Local legend has it that 400 years later a ploughman uncovered the Saint's grave in a field and later that day St. Ivo appeared to another man in a vision telling him that he wished his body to be removed from the ground. In due course it was taken to Ramsey Abbey and a health-giving spring is said to have arisen at the site of the grave. Slepe was renamed St. Ives in his honour.

As the river leaves St. Ives it swings north to begin its journey across the Fens towards the sea. The character of the Ouse remains much the same, a broad stately stream which seems unimpressed by everything it encounters. But there are surprises ahead for man has taken a hand and often drastically altered the course of the river to suit his own particular purposes and needs.

The old bridge and its chapel, St. Ives

Cambridge News

Chapter Four

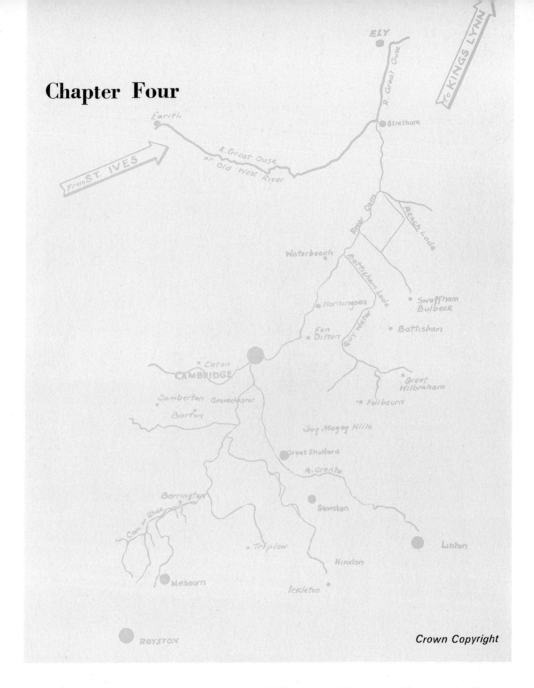

NOW that the Ouse has become completely navigable it would seem sacrilege to continue other than upon its broad highway. From Cambridge to the Wash and from Huntingdonshire across to the borders of Suffolk there are literally hundreds of miles of waterways to explore in any one of the many well-equipped motor launches that are available on hire from various centres. Each year an increasing number of people find pleasure on this river.

One does not have to become an experienced yachtsman or navigator before setting out. In fact the greater fun comes from starting such an adventure in the company of the family or friends and just setting off to learn as you go. It was thus that I and a companion, whose profession as well as interest in life was photography, once set out to write about and photograph the various waterways of the Ouse.

Our boat, a neat cruiser with two cabins, was obtained from Banham's Cambridge boat yard and we boarded her as she lay opposite the grey mass of the city's gas works. It was complete with blankets, cutlery and linen all neatly stowed and the appropriate tanks filled with fuel and water. A cheery man gave us a short lecture on the engine and its requirements. He continued the lesson with a short run up the river and back to make certain that we had a passable understanding of the craft and knew which lever meant forward and which obtained reverse—two directional movements which we, with a nautical air, soon referred to as ahead and astern.

In many ways it was all rather reminiscent of the early days of motoring when the roads were uncluttered and the beginner still had room to make mistakes without disaster to himself or others. We questioned our tutor about the way in which the boats were operated. He told us that his firm had a fleet of over 25 boats afloat each season on a weekly hire basis, and that they went out on Saturday afternoon to return at the end of the timed period, be it for one or more weeks, on a Saturday morning. This left them with something like four hours in which to strip completely each of the boats, refuel, rewater, carry out minor repairs, clean the boat from stem to stern and generally have it ready for the next customer.

As part of their service they provided a detailed map of the navigable rivers which was marked with petrol, telephone and water points and a mass of other detail; many other firms offer a reasonably similar service and it is possible to hire various types of craft both by the day and by the hour. Our instructor seemed satisfied with our progress and hopped briskly ashore as we slowed down by the slipway. We carried out an effective but rather untidy three point turn in the river while he regarded us with some amusement from the shore. We opened up the throttle, pointed our bow towards Ely and the Fens and were away.

The Cam has been described as a ditch above the city of Cambridge and a sewer on the other side, but however accurate the description may have been in the past, nothing could be further from the truth these days. Some miles downstream from Cambridge at the "Fish and Duck" corner the Cam flows into the Ouse. One tributary of the Cam, the River Rhee, however starts many miles upstream from the famous University city in a most dramatic way at that most picturesque of villages, Ashwell.

Here a series of springs run from a steep hillside and set the scene for a most intriguing biological curiosity and one which has been the subject of much argument and discussion in recent years. This is the famous Ashwell worm, Crenobia Alpina to the knowledgeable, which has lived in the pool formed by the springs ever since the Ice Age. The water of the springs is a constant 52 degrees as it emerges from the ground and stays at about this figure in both winter and summer. The worm needs a fairly constant temperature in which to survive, and survive it has for all these years.

Crenobia Alpina is not found elsewhere and is of great importance to scientists at the Cambridge University Department of Zoology. There was considerable consternation when the Lee Valley Water Company proposed to pump water from the stream, because it was known that there was a chance that the worm would die out and this important but tenuous living link with one of the great ages of the world's history would disappear. But a public inquiry resulted in certain safeguards being imposed over the pumping and the future of Crenobia Alpina now seems reasonably secure.

From the Ice Age Crenobia Alpina have inhabited these Ashwell springs   *Cambridge News*

"Stands the Church clock at ten to three?"

asked Rupert Brooke in his poem "The Old Vicarage, Grantchester". To-day, as this picture shows, the Grantchester Church clock is no longer stopped but locally one can find "honey still for tea".

Cambridge News

A waterborne traffic problem on the Backs at Cambridge. That in the streets is worse!

Cambridge News

From its interesting beginnings the Rhee flows on to even more interesting surroundings. At Grantchester, an exceptionally pretty village just outside Cambridge and famous for its associations with the poet Rupert Brooke, the river joins the Cam. This attractive little river splits in two some miles to the east at Stapleford, with one branch called the Granta* running up to Linton while the Cam itself runs to the south through Saffron Walden. It is this stream which runs through the grounds of Audley End House, a superb stately early 17th century mansion which is now in the care of the Ministry of Works and which houses some very valuable paintings including a number of Canalettos.

*Many contend that Granta was the true and original name of the river and that Cam was the name that only came into usage about 1600. In Frank Rutter's excellent guide to Cambridge, revised by F. Brittain, Litt. D., a Fellow of Jesus College and published by W. Heffer and Sons Ltd., an explanation of this is given. We are told that it was derived from the name of the town by people who had forgotten its origin: "Grantabridge" hardened into "Cantabridge" which in turn softened into Cambridge.

Cambridge is famous as a University city but to visitors from every part of the world it is probably the river scenery as the Cam flows through the famous "Backs" which remains longest in their memories. There isn't much that one can write about it which has not already been said apart from the fact that the gardens, walks, terraces, bridges and collections of plants and trees backed by the full majesty of the college and University buildings add up to the most superb half mile scene in the whole of Europe, if not in the world. Man and nature working together in perfect harmony and sympathy. The "Backs" to which the name refers is that of the various Cambridge colleges. From Silver Street, where punts and boats may be hired, the river passes Queen's College, flows under King's Bridge, on to King's College and its famous chapel. Then comes Clare Bridge, but make no extravagant bets as to the number of stone balls decorating its top—a slice has been cut from one of them. Between this bridge and that of Garret Hostel stands Clare College and Trinity Hall and then Trinity College with its own bridge. There are two bridges to St. John's College and one of these is the well known copy of the famous Venetian Bridge of Sighs.

"The Backs" end just beyond St. John's College at Magdalene College (pronounced Maudalin in Cambridge and Magdalain in Oxford). This is just the other side of a road bridge bearing the same name. Here again boats and punts may be hired. A short distance down stream from this point is Jesus Green lock, the highest point on the Cam from which our motor launch could start on its voyage of exploration of the Ouse and its upper tributaries.

A canal barge acts as a house boat on the Cam at Cambridge   *Cambridge News*

Through Fen Ditton and Horningsea, names well known to the rowing men of Cambridge, my companion and I chugged in our newly acquired floating home. Our maps showed that just ahead we were about to meet our first lock of the trip, that at Baits Bite, so we decided to moor alongside the bank and plan how we would tackle the situation. My crew of one adopted a suitably nautical pose on the right hand (or is it starboard?) side of the boat and flung out a hand with the air of Columbus sighting America. "That's the place" he said, "an ideal parking spot to tarry a while and ponder".

I was in charge of the wheelhouse. As I eased back on the throttle and hauled the large gear lever into neutral the crew grabbed the boathook and made a few professional looking passes at an overhanging willow. Slowly the boat came to a halt in midstream. I grappled with reverse gear. Reverse gear engaged, throttle open, a few brisk twirls on the wheel and the boat responded by placing itself sideways across the stream.

We stared at each other, each mirroring the disbelief of individuals brought up on the motor vehicle, and then flung ourselves back into our respective tasks. Throttle open, throttle closed. Reverse, forward, reverse again. Thrust and parry with the boathook and there we were—boat facing in the opposite direction. Fantastic!

Fortunately there was no one watching but in the event of there having been I had already laid plans for sailing back up stream with all the nonchalance of hardened experts who had planned just such a manoeuvre. As it was we were faced with turning the boat about and continuing with our seemingly simple plan of parking alongside a grassy bank. It seemed an eternity before we had the bow of the boat again pointing toward Ely but eventually we were moving gently once more in the right direction. Slowly we bore down on our selected spot, boathook at the ready, gears and throttle nursed into harmony. Suddenly the nose of the boat rose gently as if lifted by a whale, the wheel kicked about as if it had decided to take matters into its own hands and the forward motion of the boat stopped—we were aground.

Much thrusting and revving later we were off the unknown shoal and nursing our pride in mid-stream. There was only one thing to do and we did it. All thoughts of making a landing were abandoned and we beat it with our landing ropes between our legs, so to speak, towards Clayhithe. There we found an excellent mooring along-side the equally excellent Bridge Hotel and made a passable job of stopping at it.

Soon we were on our way and into the next lock. It is against the various locks on the river that the beginner in the art of handling a motor cruiser can judge his pro-gress. The first lock is an inevitable ordeal. There is no opportunity to go away quietly and practice beforehand, one rounds a bend in the river and there it is. We found that more often than not the lock gates are closed and there is a wait while the lock keeper fills up the lock and opens the gates for the craft to enter. I soon discovered that the problem lies in knowing what to do in the meantime. If it is obviously going to take some time we found it better to remain moored at the bank before steering an S shaped course into the mouth of the lock. If on the other hand the lock gates were about to open it is possible to reduce speed and maintain just enough way on to keep the craft under control. Occasionally the current would play funny tricks and the nose of the boat would begin to move sideways. Eventually we mastered the art of putting the boat astern and holding it on the rudder. We even worked out a technique for using rudder, throttle and gears in unison to bring the boat into the bank sideways, a performance which came in useful when mooring space was limited.

The Backs as they are remembered by men and women the world over
Cambridge News

Wherever we went up and down the Ouse and its many tributaries each lock, with the exception of the most remote, seemed to attract a selection of Fenland worthies whose sole occupation is that of leaning on the arms of the lock gate, pipe in teeth and accompanied by a dog on a piece of string. Their sole interest in life appeared to be that of assessing the skill of the various crews using the locks. They flinch with you if an unfendered piece of boat happens to touch the sides, they commiserate with the lock keeper if he points out somewhat briskly that you should be hanging onto the chains at the edges but they stare impassively if by superb seamanship you check an almost suicidal move on the part of the craft.

One onlooker who has mixed feelings about motor craft on the river is the angler. Talking to a number of them at various times I have discovered that there is, unhappily, a large proportion of people on board cruisers who make no effort to slow down if they encounter a fishing match in progress.

The Old West River, which the Cam joins at "Fish and Duck" corner north of Cambridge, is a somewhat narrow and winding stream at the best of times, and here one angling club tends to suffer a great deal from interference from motor cruisers. Not only do the boats often pass at too high a speed but some particularly selfish and ignorant elements deliberately steer for the fishing bank only to swing away at the last minute. Sometimes a Fenman's reaction to this lack of consideration is to hurl a handful of maggots on board as the boat goes by. Some time later these hatch into magnificent bluebottles to plague the selfish occupants of the boat!

In many cases antagonism can occur through sheer thoughtlessness on the part of people in boats, especially those who are merely holidaying on the waters and do not have a permanent interest in establishing and maintaining good and happy relations with others who enjoy the countryside, the banks and meadows. For me the river is a place of immense peace and solitude and it seems altogether wrong that it should sometimes unwittingly form the background for angry feelings. It has its own moods and changing atmosphere and a particular smell of its own which is not in the least unpleasant. In the background, like a musical accompaniment, are the gentle sough of wind through the grass and reeds, the murmur of water lapping against boat and banks, the cry of birds and the melody of many other pleasant river sounds.

Another important characteristic lies in a different dimension. Life on the river completely alters one's concept of time. Most people find that after only a short period afloat they have lost all track of time. The fact that a journey which would take minutes by car must of necessity take hours, introduces a restfulness which is almost impossible to obtain elsewhere in this bustling world. Hurry and rush are sapped out of existence by the very size and pace of a slow moving mass of water. To induce it to go faster is unthinkable and to rush in its presence is out of the question. All this tends to accentuate the artificiality of modern life and the broad, wide open, unpeopled expanses of the Fens make it quite clear that the noisy overcrowding of suburbia is something for which man alone is responsible, much to his discredit.

Magdalene Bridge, Cambridge   *Cambridge News*

A typical Fenland village, Cottenham, Cambridgeshire

R. Tibbs

Chapter Five

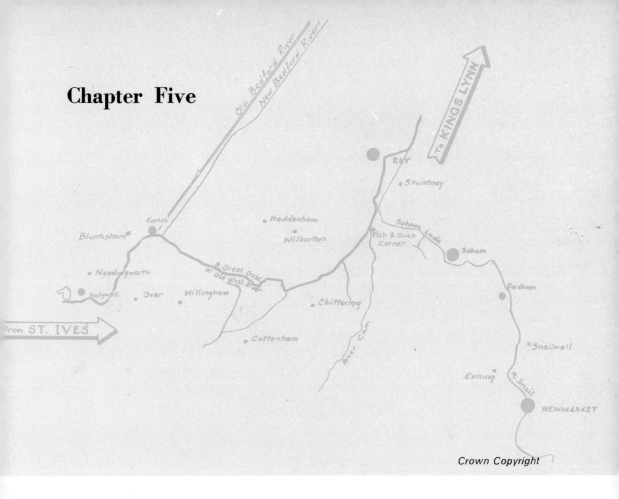

WHEN I first encountered the Fish and Duck, at the junction of the Ouse with the Old West River just below Ely, it was a charming, rather tumbledown old pub which, like many Fenland buildings, had long since ceased to stand up straight. The name survives but on a completely new building. It offers excellent moorings, meals and snacks and is an ideal point at which to "heave to" at the end of a day's journey on the river.

Fish and Duck corner has seen some tough times. The earlier landlord, who ran the old establishment, recalled for me the famous winter of 1962 when the river was frozen solid between the pub and Ely. Supplies of beer and provisions were brought out by sledge along the river surface and skaters found it a hospitable source of warmth, jollity and comfort after a similar journey upstream. Reaching the pub by land was completely out of the question since deep drifts effectively marooned the place. At the best of times it is difficult to get there by road and once involved a most odd journey across numerous Fenland fields and a railway line. The journey has since been shortened but is still unusual.

Old Inn

M. Manni

FISH AND DUCK

New Inn

Ely Standard

We cruised westward along the winding track of the Old West. This river formed the original course of the Ouse from Earith across to Ely before man, in the form of Vermuyden and the Bedford Adventurers, started drainage work. Today it is quite navigable and gives helmsmen plenty to do as it swings first this way and that. On either side are wide, lush, welcoming meadows, every one of them a splendid anchoring point. At the far end stands Hermitage Lock, a natural gateway both to the New Bedford River running north and to the Ouse as it passes through Earith and the Hemingfords to Huntingdon. The old lock at Hermitage was a creaky but picturesque affair and one had to apply to the lock keeper in his nearby cottage for a passage through. Now major reconstruction work has been undertaken as the result of which the lock keeper's cottage stands in more modern surroundings a little distance from the lock itself.

We paused for a while at Earith and here discovered that for some years the post master has operated an amateur radio station alongside the counter. It is a hobby and one which has come in very useful in times of flood and disaster. Through Brownshill Staunch, a modern lock with "guillotine" like action, we chugged on until we came to one of the finest stopping places throughout the entire length of the Ouse, the anchorage by the Ferry Boat at Holywell not far from St. Ives. The village is charming and was once a busy port for the river trade between Bedford and Kings Lynn. Today it still has a waterfront atmosphere about parts of it and Anchor Cottage, not far from the Ferry Boat, was once the Anchor Inn.

Holywell gained itself some extra acres when the river changed its direction to a more southerly course some time in the fourteenth century. The old river bed can still be seen in the meadows by anyone with a sharp eye and a gift for such things. Holywell gets its name from a well in the churchyard which has holy associations. The church was mentioned in the Domesday Survey and the well is still trickling away today. The Rev. R. S. Beckwith fitted it with a little stone arch in 1847 and this remains in good repair. The Rev. Pearce Higgins, when he was incumbent, told me that a few years back the spring was cleaned out and it was found to have three shillings and six pence in coppers at the bottom. Some visitors, it seems, are convinced that it is a wishing well and throw in a coin or two before making a wish.

The Ferry Boat itself is a magnificent old inn which lays claim to the title of the oldest inn in Great Britain. It is listed as among the oldest by the Guinness Book of Records but I have been unable to substantiate this. The thatched end, that is in fact the oldest part, of the present inn dates back to about 1500 and it is almost certain that an inn stood on the spot for a long time before that, but documentary records are difficult to come by. It is reputed to be haunted and the barman tells alarming stories of mugs and bottles flying about. The cynics argue that these are simply good tales told to encourage business. The pub is also reputed to be associated with Hereward the Wake, but again I have been unable to find any reference to Holywell village in Hereward writings. "Des Cestis Herewardi Saxonis" (The Exploits of Hereward the

The holy well in the churchyard at Holywell   *R. Tibbs*

Saxon) from an original manuscript contained in a book compiled by Robert of Swaffham is now in the possession of the Dean and Chapter of Peterborough. This interesting document is almost certainly the oldest piece of writing about Hereward and describes a number of his adventures about the river. It is known that he lived in the woods in Northamptonshire and I would think it highly likely that Hereward used the river ford at Holywell for a number of crossings into and out of the Fens—but again it is difficult to find documentary evidence. Holywell is not mentioned by name even though a number of places are detailed in the manuscript.

The thatched and oldest end of the Ferry Boat Inn, Holywell. It has associations with Hereward the Wake and listed as one of the oldest in the country   *R. Tibbs*

Moorings at the Ferry Boat Inn, Holywell

M. Manni

We moored for the night at Holywell and as my companion bustled about preparing the evening meal I used the limited space in the galley as an excuse to take a seat and stay out of his way. We fell to musing about the oddities of life on a cruiser. As newcomers to the game we found that the whole experience provided a never ending round of amusing novelties. From inside the cruiser we viewed life through small, round, nine inch diameter portholes. We found it difficult to cook or eat a meal with the distraction of a large tuft of grass sliding backwards and forwards, up and down and visible through a porthole just above the cooker. As the grass carried out this perpetual and intricate sliding movement the eggs in the frying pan would set up a complementary slithering as if they were joining in some form of weird, inanimate dance.

The plumbing system not only removed the endless humping and carrying of water I associate with caravan life but it provided us with a never ending source of intellectual challenge and entertainment. Each tap developed a distinct personality of its own. Two were slightly "up" on their fellows. These were clearly labelled "Fresh

Anchor Cottage, in the centre of the picture, was once the Anchor Inn. It served the waterfront when rivermen thronged the Ouse at Holywell   *R. Tibbs*

Water" and were supplied from different sources. The tap over the little galley sink had the word "Whale" stamped on its knob, and this was fed from a tank under the wheelhouse floor. It was operated by plunging the knob of the tap up and down, an operation which caused my companion accidentally to ricochet water from an obliquely held plate all over himself on more than one occasion. The other fresh water tap was fed from a front mounted tank in the bow and had a habit of performing a little extra dribble of water after the operator had turned his back. We even tried playing a waiting game with it, but it always won.

Two further taps, one in a small sink in the galley and another in the tiny toilet had a musical accompaniment. By pressing down on the operating knob one could get a whirring sound from the bowels of the boat which we deduced to be from some form of electrical pump. These two were very temperamental. Sometimes they worked, sometimes not. We cured this by playing one off against the other. A short burst on the one in the bow fooled the one in the toilet into providing water, and vice versa. But they had the last laugh. We cleaned our teeth from the one in the toilet before we discovered that it received its water direct from the river outside!

Riverside scene at Ely   *M. Manni*

The Cutter Inn at Ely

D. Monk by courtesy Ely Standard

Water also behaved oddly in the metal sink in the galley. Depending upon the angle of the boat there was always a small amount in the bottom which refused to go away. We worked out a system of moving everyone on the boat to one side. This had the effect of providing just the right degree of tilt to drain the water out, a dodge which mystified visitors and onlookers alike, but which nevertheless was very effective.

I am sure that the scientists of the psychology departments of nearby Cambridge University would have found some very useful practical environmental material in our general behaviour on board. My length of six feet provided me with a few problems and I experienced my share of bumped heads and damaged elbows. One would have thought that our crew of one, with his height of five feet and five and a half inches would have suffered less, but no. His speciality was crashing his head on the coaming over the entrance to the rear cabin. He would then slowly totter across the wheelhouse floor in a semi-conscious state, head reeling and with stars before his eyes, prior to falling two feet down into the front cabin to end up with a crash on the dining table. There was what the scientists would call a marked lack of environmental response. He repeated the performance again and again.

We both had trouble with knots. We longed for the time when we could jump from a craft at a mooring, perform a number of deft twists on the bow and stern lines and know in our hearts that the boat was completely safe. Once we thought we had brought it off—but it was not to be. Ourselves and a group of worthies outside the Cutter Inn at Ely stared in amused disbelief as our briskly tied knots slowly untied themselves like nylon snakes waking up in the morning. To cope with this our knots became enormous conglomerations of twists and turns which threatened to rival the complexity of the knotted rope fenders which hung along the side of the boat. The strength of our ropework lay in the sheer length of time it took for each knot to untie itself, loop by loop, under the constant pull of the moored craft.

For as long as we stayed on the boat we found ourselves discovering new cupboards and storage places. A piece of panelling with some holes in it would turn out to be a door. There were hatches and lockers in the most unlikely places and every nook and cranny turned out to contain its special surprises. I would not like this read in any way as a complaint against the boat or the joys of boating. The foregoing incidents are included merely as illustration of the pure fun and entertainment which can be found by anyone keen to enjoy themselves on the waterways of the Great Ouse.

Ely is an important spot when cruising on the river. Often in the somewhat featureless areas of the Fens when we were a little lost for direction we found that by standing on the cabin roof we could sooner or later pick out the towering height of Ely cathedral somewhere in the distance and thus take our bearings. On a clear day it is possible to see the cathedral from Cambridge, over sixteen miles away. It certainly dominates the entire Fen landscape and becomes a reassuring and friendly mass to anyone moving about in the region. To-day with modern communications and road systems it is not easy to get lost in the Fens. This was not always so and it is interesting to note that the Curfew Bell of Great St. Mary's Church, Cambridge, was rung each evening—its friendly voice sent echoing across the Fens to act as a guide to the travellers in the Fenlands who were within earshot.

Appleyard & Lincoln, well known for the "Elysian" class cruisers which they build, have their boatyard and headquarters at Ely. They can supply anything that the riverborne traveller may require in the boating line. The firm have modernised their premises in recent years and now have splendid docking and slipway facilities.

Just across the river from this boatyard is a beautiful little riverside scene centred around the Cutter Inn. Petrol is available here for cruisers and there is refreshment for the crew. If there is any shopping to be done it is but a short walk, up charming little narrow streets, into the City itself. Ely has long been a City but it was only in

Ely Cathedral—*Cambridge News* ▶

recent years that a City Charter was granted to Cambridge. The Isle of Ely has been called "the heart of the Fenland". It became a division of Cambridgeshire in 1892 having earlier been a Liberty. In 1888 The Isle became an administrative County and operated as such until 1st April 1965 when Cambridgeshire and the Isle of Ely became one county.

Ely really was an Isle in the days before the Fens were drained. The routes in and out of it were few and far between and it was by the skilful use of the island and marshes that Hereward the Wake was able to hold out so long and so effectively against William the Conquerer.

St. Etheldreda, who was born at Exning near Newmarket in about 630 A.D., started in 673 A.D. to build a Minster at Ely. This was sacked by the Danes in 870 A.D., but was reconsecrated a century later and by the coming of the Normans was certainly one of the mightiest in the country. It was due to the treachery of the Monks of Ely that William I was able to find a way through the Fens to attack and break up Hereward's camp. Although Hereward escaped it had denied him a wonderful natural fortress.

To the student of architecture Ely Cathedral to-day provides excellent examples of many differing styles of architecture. These include Norman (11th and 12th century), Early English (13th century), Decorated (14th century), Perpendicular (15th and early 16th century) and post Reformation (late 16th century on). One famous feature is the 14th century Octagon, an enormous eight sided lantern, the incredible tonnage of which is entirely supported on downward thrusting wooden beams. Looking at it from inside one can but appreciate what a wonderful engineering and architectural achievement this was as indeed is the entire building. Couple this with the beauty of its glass and general appearance and one must hold in high regard the designers, architects and engineers of long ago and praise their superb skill. The Fens are notoriously bad at supporting any large weight and most Fen houses tend to lean a bit as they sink into the soft unstable sub-soil. The Cathedral however was built by people who knew what they were about and in spite of the enormous weight it is to-day still as upright as ever—and they did not have modern methods of placing the foundations on huge concrete piles.

It is thought that Oliver Cromwell, who lived in Ely for a time, may have saved the Cathedral from much of the damage sustained by churches in that period. Some damage did occur and is still visible, but it is nothing compared with that inflicted on many East Anglian churches and perpetrated under the evil direction of William Dowsing.

It is interesting to note that one small area in London, Ely Place, was the site of the London home of former Bishops of Ely. Situated at Holborn Circus it is a private street and, under a special Act of Parliament, its affairs are administered by Commissioners.

This beautiful house at Haddenham bears traces of Dutch influence in its design

R. Tibbs

Chapter Six

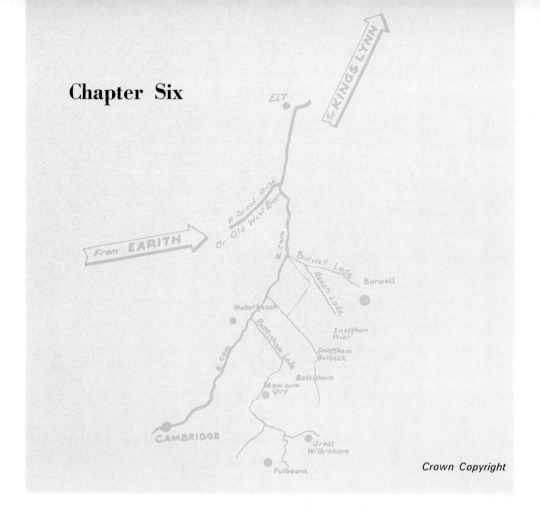

THE drainage of the Fens and its long and adventurous history forms a separate chapter of this book. We should however, now that we are in Fen country, note the flat and somewhat featureless scenery, the vast skies and recall a little of the past. Apart from its flatness, which is obvious to all, there is another characteristic which, although obvious when pointed out, more often than not passes unnoticed by the visitor.

To-day the Fens are one of the few parts of the world where the rivers run *above* the level of the surrounding countryside. The Ouse from its junction with the Old West to many miles beyond Ely runs between huge flood banks and the level of the water within the banks is actually above the meadows. Even the tributaries, including the Wissey, the Lark and the Little Ouse all exhibit the same strange idiosyncrasy. We may well ask if the rivers and ground started on level terms after which the land sank, or did the rivers, for some mysterious reason, rise above their surroundings?

It was the rivers which remained put and the land which dropped, and the explanation gives us the key to a problem which continues in the Fens—one for which an answer is still to be found. When waterlogged peat soil, such as is found in the Fens, is drained there is considerable shrinkage which can amount to as much as 6 inches or so a year. If the surface of the land drops by this amount the temptation is to lower still further the water level in order to overcome the resulting unsatisfactory drainage and as a result there is yet more sinking. These were mistakes which were made at various times in the early days of Fen drainage and they also did not take into account a further problem. There is a gradual surface wastage of dry peat, sometimes hastened by the action of the sun and high winds, and accelerated by oxidisation. The lowering of the land surface resulted in bad drainage and eventually it was necessary to raise banks alongside the rivers to contain them and to effect drainage by lifting the water up into the streams. Gradually there came about a total separation of the river system from the drainage system, and, although most people automatically assume that Fen water drains into the rivers by gravity, in fact this hardly ever occurs. The rivers normally flow between six and twelve feet above the Fens behind their flood banks and give the area its present characteristic appearance. Special research is being carried out at the Arthur Rickwood farm at Mepal by government departments into this particular problem. Alderman Rickwood left the farm to the nation on his death in recent years for just such a purpose. "The Carrot King" was the title fondly applied to him during his highly successful career as a Fen farmer in recognition of the crop which first set him on the path to a respectable fortune.

If anyone doubts that the Fens are shrinking they should go to Holme Fen where proof may be found of shrinkage of nearly 13 feet since 1848. This was recorded on what was known as the Holme Fen Post of which most if not all of the published details are inaccurate. I am indebted to Mr. W. E. Doran for an interesting and accurate account of this famous post. What happened was that in 1848, prior to the draining of the Fen three timber piles were driven in. Mr. Doran continues "The next chapter in the story is a visit to the Great Exhibition of 1851 by the landowners interested which resulted in the purchase of the Appold pump—the first centrifugal pump to be used for fen drainage. When the exhibition buildings were being taken down, I presume, a cast iron column was purchased and this is the Holme Fen Post. In reference to it in H. C. Darby's "Draining of the Fens" and elsewhere it is said that in 1851 the iron post was sunk to the solid clay. About 1958 it came to my notice that the post was unsteady and could be rocked by hand. I was worried about this. Then the Nature Conservancy took over this part of the fen and ultimately it was agreed that a new post should be erected."

Mr. Doran said that the Engineer to the Middle Level, a Mr. L. F. Fillenham, drove a concrete pile down into the clay and on top of this erected a cast iron lamp post. The Nature Conservancy then dug down and found that the original post was cracked and that it rested on a cast iron base, in the shape of a cross with one long member in the centre of which was a circle from which two short arms protruded at right angles to form the cross. This base in turn rested on some filling and thus it appeared that the post did not go down to the clay and measurements were thus likely to be inaccurate.

The story continues in Mr. Doran's own words "Subsequently Fillenham made a further investigation and found that in fact the base rested upon a timber pile, so in fact the shrinkage measurements could be relied upon after all. This pile is probably one of the three originally driven in 1848. The post was not driven down, it was put in with its base by excavating. So here is the history of the Holme Fen Post to date!"

It was shortly after the original shrinkage of the Fens became apparent that mechanical methods of effecting drainage by lifting water into the river were introduced. At first windmills were used for this purpose and the Fenland regions must have looked even more like the countryside of Holland than they do now. The mills usually drove huge scoop wheels which worked in a brick trough outside the mill. They were only really effective when the wind blew at a speed greater than about twelve miles an hour but the method was not without its problems. Often the waters would rise when the wind was light and sometimes it blew hard when the tide was already high in the Wash and the mills had to stop pumping.

Windpower was superseded by steam and at Stretham, just by the Old West River, the visitor can still see a magnificently preserved example of a beam engine which last pumped water in earnest in 1941. The engine is preserved and administered by the Stretham Engine Preservation Trust and the engine house is open to the public. Once inside this gaunt building it is not difficult to imagine the past. Everything is much as it was when the last engineer departed. His oil cans, lathe, spanners, the nuts, bolts, wire and assorted oddments of a lifetime spent tending machinery still lie on the window ledges and benches. His work must have been rather precarious. When the enormous engine with its 23ft. flywheel was chugging away in times of flood he had to make a tour of the building oiling the machinery at least once every hour throughout the day and night. This involved climbing numerous small stone steps, some of them high above the engine room floor with only an oil lamp to light the way.

Today the Preservation Trust have installed metal railings and made the building as safe to visitors as they can. On the very top floor is a small but interesting collection of Fenland relics, which include examples of bog oak—early black oak from the forest that once covered the region which has been preserved in the peat — and bones of animals now extinct in this part of the world.

Anyone who has an interest in the past will find many places, not far from the banks of the Ouse and its connecting rivers, where the history of the region is not preserved in a museum but where it exists in a living form and in a way which is quite startling and unique. At Wicken the Cam flows past Wicken Fen, one of the first possessions

Old windmill from Adventurers Fen re-erected at Wicken Fen—*R. Tibbs* ▶

acquired by the National Trust and an area of Fenland which is really virgin fen. When the "Adventurers" started draining the Fens the newly acquired land was measured out and parcelled off for cultivation. But Wicken Fen was left as common land for the people of Wicken village but the villagers neither drained nor cultivated it.

Consequently when we look at Wicken Fen today, and it is open to visitors, we are really looking at Fenland as it must have looked hundreds of years ago. In fact if one stands opposite Monk's Lode—one of the ancient water ways cut for the transport of peat—and looks south across Wicken Lode one can see that the level of the whole of the Fenlands to the south is six to eight feet below the level of the centre of the Wicken Fen area. This represents the shrinkage mentioned earlier. Just across Wicken

View at Wicken Fen   R. *Tibbs*

Reed cutter's boats and stack of thatching reeds, Wicken Fen   *R. Tibbs*

Lode can be seen old bog oaks taken out of the peat when Adventurers' Fen was reclaimed for agriculture during the last war.

Also at Wicken Fen is a fine example of a drainage windmill of the type first used to lift water up into the rivers. It came from Adventurers' Fen where it had become derelict and while the woodwork has been restored the ironwork is original. There is much to see at Wicken for the place abounds in wildlife—there is a specially constructed mere with an observation hide: indeed here can be found flora and fauna of all kinds in wild duck, rare butterflies and moths with Montagu's harriers all mid meadowsweet, sedge and reeds. It is also used for a considerable amount of experimental work and in Sedge Fen Drove* one can see some of this in progress. Here are a set of five experimental plots of sedge set out by Professor Godwin in 1927 to study the effects of mowing sedge at varying intervals. The first enclosure is mown annually, the second every two years and so on. The fifth and last is never touched and acts as a 'control'. In another part of the Fen some oak trees have established themselves and a wood is developing. It is believed that if the Fen was left completely alone an oak and ash forest would eventually cover most of it. And who knows, this might again take on the appearance of the countryside as it might have looked thousands of years ago in prehistoric times.

Not so very far away and approximately half way between the Ouse at St. Neots and the Cam at Grantchester is a piece of woodland which is as original in its way as Wicken Fen. This is Hayley Wood at Longstowe owned by the Cambridge Naturalist Trust. It represents a piece of original deciduous forest cover of the sort which originally spread throughout East Anglia and many other parts of England. This also is open to the visitors and is the subject of experiment. At Wicken Fen it appears that without disturbance the woodland would revert to oak and ash but in the centre of Hayley Wood is an area where drainage is poor and large pools of water lie for long periods in the winter. Here oak and ash do not do so well but Salix cinerea, a form of willow, thrives. One of the long term aims at Hayley Wood is to leave the waterlogged area untouched to see what finally succeeds in growing there.

In other parts of the wood a form of rotational cutting and replanting practised since mediaeval times is continuing and naturalists are making an intensive study of the types of wild flowers which follow in the wake of such a programme and its effects upon animal life.

Bottisham Lode† empties itself into the Cam just below Bottisham Lock, itself not far from Wicken Fen. The Lode, an ancient drainage and transport waterway, runs up to Lode village and a fine old water mill before swinging south into the grounds of Anglesey Abbey, which can be reached by water. Few people knew much about the Abbey until the death of its owner, Lord Fairhaven in 1966. Queen Elizabeth the Queen Mother was among his friends and she stayed at the Abbey on one or two occasions but the house had never been opened to the general public and visitors were few. Lord Fairhaven argued that to open the house to one person would rightly mean opening it to all and he did not wish his home to become just another stately house. But on his death, and at his wish, all this was changed for he left Anglesey Abbey and its 1,000 acres with £300,000 for its upkeep to the National Trust. When the Trust came to survey the property they realised that they had not inherited "just another stately home" but one of the most staggering private art collections in the world.

They have never been able to put a price on it for the work of valuation would take experts so long that by the time they had finished their task market values would

*The term "drove" means a green road in the Fenlands.
†The term "lode" applies mainly to the Fens and describes an artificial channel or water-course, most of which are embanked.

Anglesey Abbey — the dormered roof line and front entrance were added by the late Lord Fairhaven

R. Tibbs

have altered. It was found that the Abbey's late owner was a man not only of considerable taste for Gainsboroughs, Claudes, Constables, Ming, jade, books and objects d'art, but that he was a gardener in the grand manner. Anglesey Abbey's acres had provided a landscape challenge which he had solved with great ingenuity. When Lord Fairhaven acquired the property in 1926, it was nothing very special and the pictures in the library to this day show that it was not in a good state of repair. He rebuilt parts of the house with such ingenuity that it now appears older than it really is and he laid out the grounds so that they provided their own natural protection against the blasting winds of the open Fenland.

Sir Arthur Bryant, the historian, has said of the Abbey grounds that they are "likely to remain the last and not the least beautiful of England's classic gardens." And this is the really important point about Lord Fairhaven's creation. Although it may appear equal to if not better than many of England's great houses and gardens it should be remembered that Anglesey Abbey has been lovingly brought up to its present magnificence in under 10 years. Visitors may wander around the Monks Garden, the Rose Garden, the Dahlia Garden, the Herbaceous Garden, the Pinetum, the Arboretum, stroll along the numerous walks or through the glades to admire the changing vistas. All this in a setting of an outstanding collection of rare trees from all parts of the world interspersed with an amazing collection of statuary. Ridges and depressions in the South Glade are formed by the foundations of the old Abbey, which was of the Augustinian Order, and by the various excavations that have been carried out for one reason or another. All round this Glade and elsewhere in the garden are deeper depressions which were originally moats or ponds for fish. These depressions dictated, in many instances, the vistas and shapes which have been laid out. If you visit the garden look for a tree called Metasequoia Glypstroboides which is in the Arboretum. They are becoming a little more common these days but it was not until a valley full was discovered in China in 1947 that anyone had seen the living tree. It was known to plant specialists through fossil remains found in various parts of the world but the tree was believed to be extinct. It is beautiful in shape and is half way between a deciduous tree and a pine in appearance. I have one in my own garden and apart from the intrinsic interest which comes from a living tree exactly similar to those of an aeon ago it is a splendid tree in its own right. It grows quickly and turns a most beautiful coppery tint before dropping its leaves in the autumn.

Lord Fairhaven collected most things in the world of art but he was remarkable for his collection of hundreds of paintings and drawings with Windsor Castle as their subject. He owned a house at Windsor for some time and his affection for the place led him to amass this most unexpected total. In 1955 two magnificent art galleries, designed by the late Sir Albert Richardson, were added to the Abbey largely to house this collection. These and other parts of the house are open to the public and are well worth a visit.

Anglesey Abbey makes a fitting conclusion to our chapter on the unusual in the Fens. Its owner, like the traditional Fenman, was self reliant and independent. He generated his own electricity at 110 volts, he pumped his own water and he ran his own sewage farm. You cannot take Fenland independence much further than that!

I have dealt only with places that are fully open for the public to visit and hope that some may surprise and intrigue many who are unfamiliar with Fenland and the wonders to be found along the Ouse and its tributaries.

Bottisham Lode as it enters Anglesey Abbey estate. The distant mill was restored and the banks carefully planted to produce this surprisingly natural effect. _R. Tibbs_

Visitors may now enjoy the wonders of Anglesey Abbey

R. Tibbs

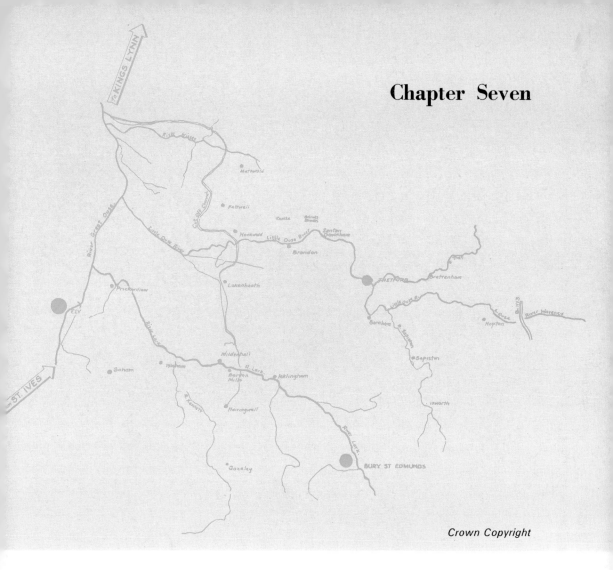

Chapter Seven

IN Fenland terms practically anything which sticks out of the ground a foot or so becomes worthy of the title "hill". There is a fair sized "range" between Haddenham and Wilburton and another parallel to it between Sutton and Ely. North Hill to the east of Haddenham in the former "range" is the highest point and reaches a staggering height of 100 feet above mean sea level. In fact a glance at the one inch Ordnance Map is interesting in that it shows a remarkable absence of contour lines. As he turns to the East the Fenman can see the distant hills of Suffolk and Norfolk, tremendous by comparison but still very low in reality. From these hills flow the four eastern tributaries of the Ouse.

These are the river Nar which strictly speaking is not a tributary because it almost reaches the Wash without assistance from the Ouse, the River Wissey, the Little Ouse

River and the River Lark. These four rivers feed into the Ouse at more or less regular intervals and they take us into country which is unlike anything the Ouse region has presented so far. For some miles from the point at which they meet the Ouse these rivers flow through true Fenland but all originate in countryside which has very different characteristics. The Lark, which is the most southerly of the four, rises in high ground at Hawstead in Suffolk and flows through Bury St. Edmunds where it is joined by the River Linnet, on to Lackford and Icklingham before passing through Mildenhall and into the Fens to meet the Ouse near Littleport. The Little Ouse takes a parallel course to the north and joins the Great Ouse at Brandon Creek. Travelling away from the Ouse it splits into two at the oddly named corner of Botany Bay from which Stallode Wash runs down towards Lakenheath. Continuing along the Little Ouse, however, we pass through Brandon, Santon Downham and to Thetford at which point it is joined by the River Thet which runs in from Shropham Fen. The source of the Little Ouse is near Redgrave and forms a watershed with the River Waveney, whose source is but a road's-width away.

Below the Little Ouse comes the River Wissey which reaches the Great Ouse just north of Ten Mile Bank. It runs through Hilgay, Stoke Ferry, Northwold and Hilborough before petering out not so very far from East Dereham. The Nar, our final tributary of the Great Ouse reaches the main river just south of Kings Lynn and travels through Narborough, West Acre, Castle Acre and a number of other small villages before reaching its source near Mileham and Tittleshall. The Lark, the Little Ouse and the Wissey are all interesting rivers to explore by boat although the degree of navigation which can be attempted in each varies to some extent.

Anyone looking for the entrance to the Lark by boat will find it about half way along the Adelaide course just below Ely. This is a three mile length of the Ouse which is ruler straight and it is used by Cambridge University for their trial eight-oared races, the results of which largely determine the university crew to meet Oxford in the annual Oxford and Cambridge boat race on the Thames. About four miles up the Lark is the village of Prickwillow which takes its name from the "pricks" or "skewers" that used to be made out of willow. The most attractive part of the Lark lies above Prickwillow and anyone in a motor boat can carry on as far as Isleham lock where the water becomes too shallow for navigation and it is only possible to continue by dinghy.

About three and a half miles further along the Ouse, travelling downstream towards Kings Lynn, is the entrance to the Little Ouse, or Brandon River as it is sometimes known. The junction is right against the Ship Inn which always used to offer an incredible choice of sandwiches—the variety ran into hundreds. About nine miles up the river one can moor at Wilton Bridge close by Lakenheath railway station. The station, incidentally, is over two miles from Lakenheath itself. Above Wilton Bridge the water is navigable by cruiser for about half a mile before it becomes too shallow. Again a

A modern problem — detergent pollution near the River Wissey   *M. Manni*

dinghy can be brought into use and there is interesting water upstream which can be explored in this way.

The Little Ouse is certainly the river for those who wish to get away from it all. The Victoria County History of Cambridgeshire points out that to the north and east of the village of Littleport is a piece of countryside said to be the loneliest spot within 100 miles of London. It includes Burnt Fen named, so legend has it, because Hereward the Wake set it on fire, and Feltwell Fen on the Norfolk side of the Little Ouse. Incidentally traces of the Beaker* people, early inhabitants of this island, have been found on an extinct course of the Little Ouse at Plantation and Peacock farms.

The river Wissey is probably the prettiest of the tributaries and its mouth, looked at as one approaches it along the Ouse, appears exceptionally narrow. This is deceptive since there is plenty of room for boats to pass and an ample depth of water. Beyond Hilgay the open meadowland gives way to woodland and the river widens near Wissing-

*Beaker people were so called from the well made and decorated beakers which they produced. Believed to have come from Spain they were traders and cattle breeders. It is thought that they dominated some late New Stone Age communities and in the early 2nd Millennium B.C. helped introduce metal work to Britain.

79

ton before narrowing again near Stoke Ferry, at which point one reaches the limit of navigation.

The presence of the Fenland leading eastward into parts of Norfolk is clearly indicated by the Domesday Book. Just about all the figures it produces for anything, plough teams, available woodland, settlements, population and so on drop dramatically once the area populated by these tributaries was reached. But on the edge of the higher ground villages were fairly frequent and sheep were numerous. The closeness of the sea during Domesday times can be gleaned from the number of saltpans recorded for the northern end of this region. The upper course of the streams and rivers, before they ran into true Fenland, seem to have been surrounded by large areas of meadow, a situation which remains much the same today.

This eastern edge of the area touched by the Ouse contains some interesting places to visit. Brandon is about the nearest bit of civilisation to the enormous American Air Force base at Lakenheath although it preserves a link with a very much older form of weaponry than that possessed by the Americans. Brandon virtually sits on flint. Most of its cottages and buildings are built of flint stone as indeed are most churches and many other buildings in East Anglia where flint was the only natural local building stone. But Brandon is still in the flint business producing flints for muzzle loading guns. These skilfully knapped flints go in large quantities to parts of Africa where the flintlock type of gun is still in much use, as well as the U.S.A. where flintlock gun societies flourish.

The Napoleonic wars were certainly fought with large quantities of flint produced at Brandon for both the French and the English bought their flints from here. I often feel that some sort of ban on the export of flints to the Continent might have made the Iron Duke's task at Waterloo a little easier!

The Neolithic flint mines known as Grimes Graves are not far from Brandon. This ancient monument is in the care of the Ministry of Works and consists of a whole series of pits or diggings from which stone age man mined his flint for arrow heads and axe blades. The title 'graves' is believed to come from the German 'graben' meaning pits and anyone who visits the spot will find over 300 chalk compressed flint pits packed close together. The underground galleries lie between 20 and 40 feet deep and there is no doubt that the place still retains a very strong atmosphere of the past. Antler horn picks and bone shovels used by these early miners and their saucer shaped oil lamps have survived and can be seen here.

The easiest way to get to Grimes Graves from Brandon is to drive along the A.1065 northwards until one sees a Ministry of Works signpost pointing the way. But I can recommend a far more interesting method of getting there on foot if you have the time — it is along a roadway which itself dates back to prehistoric times. This is the Shakers Road which crosses the B.1106 about two miles south of Brandon. One can walk along

The Ship Inn, Brandon Creek   *M. Manni*

this ancient trackway and then skirt north by High Lodge hostel, a Forestry Commission depot, to reach the B.1107, Brandon-Thetford Road. The track crosses this and continues on into the village of Santon Downham—a famed local beauty spot—where there is still a ford across the Little Ouse river. From the north bank of the river the track leads straight to Grimes Graves.

Thetford, which sits astride the Little Ouse, is a charming little town busily engaged on a programme of industrial expansion, again assisted by the Greater London Council. There are new houses and factories but Thetford seems to have set itself some high architectural standards and, given a few years in which to grow into the landscape, the additions at Thetford should enhance the scenery. In this area the Little Ouse and further north the Wissey run through thick forestry lands, tended by the Forestry Commission, but it has not always been like this. Our old friend Defoe who visited this area in the eighteenth century recalled that the area was "full of open plains, somewhat sandy and barren and feeding great flocks of sheep". He was obviously describing the Brecklands of the Norfolk and Suffolk border, a part of which is now under afforestation. Of these dense pine forests the largest is Thetford Chase with 30,900 acres.

Early morning mist at the junction of the Little and Great Ouse

M. Manni

There was a time when it and Thetford Warren were thick with rabbits but myxomatosis altered all that a few years ago. The appearance of the forest land will change again in the future for in some parts the pine trees are simply providing sheltered conditions for a number of hardwoods including oak and beech. Once these are established the 'nurse' trees will come down and oak and beech forests will flourish instead.

To the south of Bury St. Edmunds the forest land has thinned out a bit, but as Thetford sits on the Little Ouse so Bury St. Edmunds sits on the Lark. Bury has always seemed to me to be a phlegmatic and essentially pleasant place which quite rightly refuses to be hurried or jostled out of its stride. I remember spending some time there a few years ago when a particularly exciting election was in progress for the parliamentary seat. Just about the only people who were showing any signs of excitement however were the candidates themselves. The people of Bury just went quietly about their business and turned out to make a suitable decision when the great day arrived.

Beodricksworth became Saint Edmund's Bury and now, to-day, Bury St. Edmunds or, more commonly in the vicinity, simply Bury. The legends that surround the young King are legion. History tells us that the Danish invaders had, for over a decade, terrorised Eastern England. The main campaigns were during the summer months and during the winter the Danes usually camped at Thetford. In 869, after a major engagement, certainly in Suffolk but claimed by some to have been at Hoxne and by others to have been Rendlesham, the King was captured. It is certain that he was brutally put to death — legend states that he was tied to an oak and used as a target by bowmen and that his head was severed and removed from his body but later the trunk and head were reunited and miraculously the body became whole again. Some 30 or more years later the mortal remains were removed from their original burial place, possibly Hoxne, and reinterred in the monastery at Beodricksworth. When Sven Forkbeard of Denmark invaded in 1010 the remains were again moved, this time to the safety of London, but soon returned to their permanent resting place which, in 1065, became St. Edmund's Bury. Many miracles are attributed to St. Edmund and Edward the Confessor held the Saint in such reverence that he always walked the last mile to the Abbey on foot. In 1041 Edward created the Franchise of the Liberty of Saint Edmundsbury which was practically identical to the County of West Suffolk as it is now. The title survives through the Coroner for the County area who is still known as Her Majesty's Coroner for the Liberty of Bury St. Edmunds.

In 1214 the Barons, disenchanted with King John, needed a secret meeting place where they might discuss what action they should take. Surrounded by Fenland, forest and marsh, reasonably remote and with the excuse of visiting the Shrine of St. Edmund — a famous centre for pilgrims since the days of Canute — the town seemed ideal. On St. Edmund's Day they made their pilgrimage and met in the Abbey Church. Here the Archbishop of Canterbury, Stephen Langton, placed before them a Charter of Liberties which was to become renowned as Magna Carta. From it sprang representational and constitutional government and so acceptable were the rights it propounded that its terms were applied in most other countries in the world. Runnymede may well be associated with Magna Carta for here it was that the document was sealed in June 1215. It was however in the Abbey Church by the banks of the Lark that Magna Carta was born and a course of action determined which was to lead to its acceptance by John on this island in the Thames.

Riverside Walk Shopping Centre, built by The Norwich Union Insurance Group at Thetford

Norwich Union

The River Lark in the Abbey Gardens, Bury St. Edmunds *Bury Free Press*

Parts of the once powerful Benedictine Abbey remain and the immaculately kept gardens form a pleasant haven for the visitor on the bank of the Lark. I can recommend the Angel Hotel opposite as an alternative haven. Standing on the Angel Hill and surrounded by some excellent and stately buildings this Inn is well furnished and a comfortable reminder to the visitor that the Cathedral town is not really as sleepy as it looks.

One of the most exciting developments in the town has been the re-opening of the old Theatre Royal which was first opened in 1819. This is heartening news when the majority of theatres are tending to close. The theatre was the scene of the world premiere of "Charley's Aunt" and closed in 1925. It then became a brewery barrel store to be re-opened with outstanding success in 1965. Theatregoers from as far away as Ipswich, Norwich and Cambridge are among its regular patrons. Formerly the theatre held a "King's licence" enabling drinks to be served in the bar until such time as the last actor left the building. It needed little to persuade some of the thespians of those days to remain as long as anyone wished to drink or those who tended the bar were prepared to serve. Such facilities are, alas, not available to-day.

The Arms of Bury St. Edmunds contain the crown and arrows of St. Edmund as well as the head of the Saint between the paws of a wolf. Legend is hereby perpetuated since it is said that the head of the Saint was lost but found by his followers some distance from the remains of his body guarded by a wolf whose howling had led them to the spot. Bury St. Edmunds is a beautiful town well worth a visit and who knows you might even be lucky enough to see "The Grey Lady" or "The Brown Monk" during one of their periodic visitations!

Inside the perimeter of the eastern tributaries of the Ouse are a number of little Fenland towns and villages all of which would merit a book in their own right. Anyone with an interest in the waterways of the Ouse will, I hope, agree that we cannot help but refer to the village of Reach which sits at the end of Reach Lode leading from the Cam to Upware. Reach was once a busy river port and in the middle ages coasters from Kings Lynn would travel up to Reach hithe to unload goods for the famous Reach fair. The odd barge carrying corn or coal came up to Reach within living memory and although this no longer happens, the fair itself continues as merrily as ever. It is held on Rogation Monday and the Mayor and Corporation of Cambridge journey, as they have done for hundreds of years, to declare it open. Pennies are thrown to the crowds of children who accumulate and the Mayor and his retinue still enjoy a memorable lunch in the village hall after the opening ceremony.

Street scene, Bury St. Edmunds

Bury Free Press

A ride through larchwoods in Thetford Chase   *Norwich Union*

But the story of Reach goes further than this. In recent years a keen amateur historian living in the village, Leonard Warren, has argued at government level that Reach is still a self-governing kingdom. He claims that King John gave the village its freedom and guaranteed it for ever in a charter signed at noon on 8th January 1201. If this is so then one can conjure up all sorts of fascinating and complicated situations involving a Kingdom within the British Isles which is entitled to self government. Imagine them abolishing income and purchase taxes and setting up a commercial radio station as a source of revenue — the idea was put up to Ronan O'Rahilly that he should move Radio Caroline into the "Kingdom". Personally if this enterprising local historian can substantiate his claim to be King or Overlord of the Ancient Kingdom of Reach I am volunteering to be its representative at the United Nations — what a thought!

Brandon Bridge over the Little Ouse

Studio Five, *Thetford*

Chapter Eight

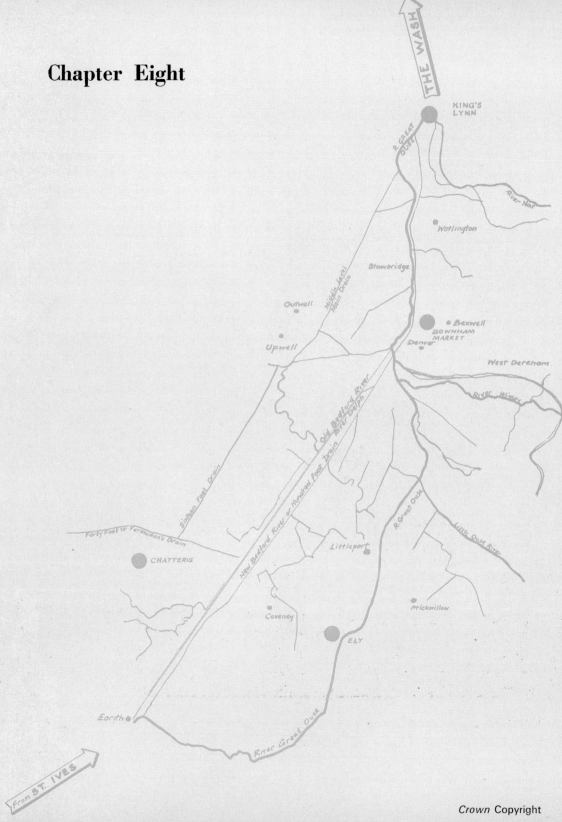

WHEN Cornelius Vermuyden and the Bedford Level Adventurers turned their attention to the Fens in 1630 they made up for their lack of money by an abundant enthusiasm. The history of Fen drainage is or has been a controversial and often violent business and one which has always been hedged about by economies of one sort or another. The scene which the Adventurers looked upon was a desolate and soggy one and the description which appears time and time again in the literature of the period, is that of "drowned lands" and seems to me to be particularly graphic.

But it was not always like that. An atlas translated by Henry Hexham and printed in Amsterdam in 1636 carries, as a title, "A description of the Drowned Lands called the Fens" in which we are transported back to the year 1200. The passage runs "They were in ancient times dry-lands and very good ground as appeareth by the history written by one William of Malmesbury who lived in the year 1200, who relateth that this country in his time was a very paradise, and seemed a heaven for the delight and beauty thereof. . . . ."

The passage goes on to refer to "Fields set with vines which either creep upon the ground or mount on high upon poles to support them for in those days there were a great store of vines in England." Hexham's own description of the scene is different and one which tells us exactly how the Adventurers saw it. Hexham says "Great plenty it hath also of turfe and sedge for the maintenance of fewell for fire; of reeds also to thatch their houses; yea and of alders besides other watery shrubs."

But who were the Bedford Level Adventurers and how did the Dutchman Vermuyden come to cut two enormous scars across the face of England? Vermuyden arrived in England in 1621 when his countryman Joachim Liens was already discussing with James I the possibility of draining the Fens. It is likely that Vermuyden came at the invitation of Liens but after a while it became clear that James, who had much on his mind at the time, was not to be hurried into a decision. Vermuyden and Liens carried out work on a breach in the banks of the Thames at Dagenham and later, when James became interested in draining the level of the Royal Chase of Hatfield, a few miles north east of Doncaster, it was natural that Vermuyden should be on hand to carry out the work. An agreement for this was signed in 1626 and it was at Hatfield that Vermuyden first demonstrated his principle of "washes".

Vermuyden argued that however good a drainage system was it would be uneconomical and too expensive if it had banks great enough to deal with the highest flood levels that might occur. A better method, he suggested, was to allow quite deliberate flooding over certain areas and thus provide somewhere in which excess water would be contained until the rest of the system could cope. In this way, he argued, the retaining banks need not be so high or so expensive. Today the land between the Old Bedford River and the New Bedford River or Hundred Foot Drain, Vermuyden's two great cuts in the Fens, are used as he intended as "wash" land — the term used to describe any land used for this sort of safety valve purpose. As recorded earlier this land is still occasionally called upon to perform just such a duty.

Many believe that it was in this thatched house at Fen Drayton that Vermuyden once lived

Cambridge News

As near as one can tell Hatfield Chase was satisfactorily drained by 1627 and the following year Vermuyden was knighted by Charles I. In 1630 the Dutchman was engaged by Francis, fourth Earl of Bedford, as Engineer and Director for the drainage of the Great Level of the Fens and from this sprang his first encounter with the Adventurers. The Earl of Bedford was interested in the drainage of the Fens for two main reasons. He owned a large tract of land in the Level and this formed part of his Thorney estate. He also saw the undertaking as a good investment for his money. With thirteen other men who joined him in this project he went ahead with plans to drain the area under the Lynn Law of 1630.* This band was called, certainly locally, The Bedford Level Adventurers.

Vermuyden was not only director of the operation but became an Adventurer in his own right. L. E. Harris in his excellent book "Vermuyden and the Fens" said "His was the master mind. He provided the plan, the thirteen other adventurers provided the money. If that plan failed, then they failed too."

The drainage work was not easy and Vermuyden and his workmen encountered numerous snags and difficulties. On many occasions the soft Fenland was against them, it would bear very little weight, and on other occasions the Fen men were against them. Many inhabitants of the Fens were perfectly happy with their way of life and were not enthusiastic about what the Earl and the Adventurers were doing. They often made things as difficult as they could, sabotaged the works and attacked the workmen.

*The 1630 Lynn Act was the parliamentary authority permitting the drainage of the Fenlands and defining the area in which work could be undertaken.

From "A description of the Drowned Lands called the Fens" translated by Henry Hexham, 1636

Cambridge University Library

OCEA-

NVS

GERMANI-

CVS,

THE GERMAIN OCEAN.

LINCOLNE SHIRE PARS

LINCOLNIÆ

HOLLAND.

MERSHE

LANDE

NORTFOLCIÆ

COMITATVS

PARS, OF NORFOLKE.

SHIRE PART OF HUNTINGTON

CANTABRIGIÆ

PARS

PART OF CAMBRIDGE

SHIRE

SUFFOLCIÆ PARS,

SUFFOLKE.

REGIONES INVNDATÆ
In partibus Comitatuum
NORFOLCIÆ, SUFFOLCIÆ,
CANTABRIGIÆ, HUNTINGTONIÆ,
NORTHAMTONIÆ, et
LINCOLNIÆ

Eventually the drainage of the Great Level was completed and the Ouse was diverted north from Earith to rejoin its original course at Denver. Under the terms of the Lynn Law the Earl of Bedford was to receive 95,000 acres of the land when drained and in due course a Commission of Sewers decreed that the land should be given to him. The decision was not very popular with his fellow Adventurers or the inhabitants. Petitions flew thick and fast and eventually King Charles took over as "undertaker" for Fen drainage himself. He increased his original share of the drained land from 1,200 acres to 152,000 acres and the Earl of Bedford had to be satisfied with 40,000 acres of land free of any liability. The original Adventurers saw very little return for their money and eventually relinquished all claims in 1638.

There was still much drainage work to be carried out in the Fens but this was held up by civil war between the Parliamentarians and Royalists which led to the execution of Charles I in 1649. But the Bedfords had not entirely faded from the picture. William, the fifth Earl of Bedford, was held by a government committee to have inherited the right to undertake drainage in the Fens, this in spite of the earlier interjection of Charles I and of two adjudications in 1637 and 1638 that the work had not been correctly carried out and that the fourth Earl was not entitled to his land.

Petitions continued to pour in from the inhabitants and land-owners but on 29th May 1649 the Commons passed an Act empowering the fifth Earl to undertake the drainage. Then followed a long period of negotiations with Vermuyden during which he hovered on the brink of becoming director of the operation once more. Vermuyden's main objection was based on a clause which the Adventurers wished to insert in his contract. This would have given them fairly close control over the manner in which he

The Delph and the Old Bedford near Mepal — two of Vermuyden's cuts   *R. Tibbs*

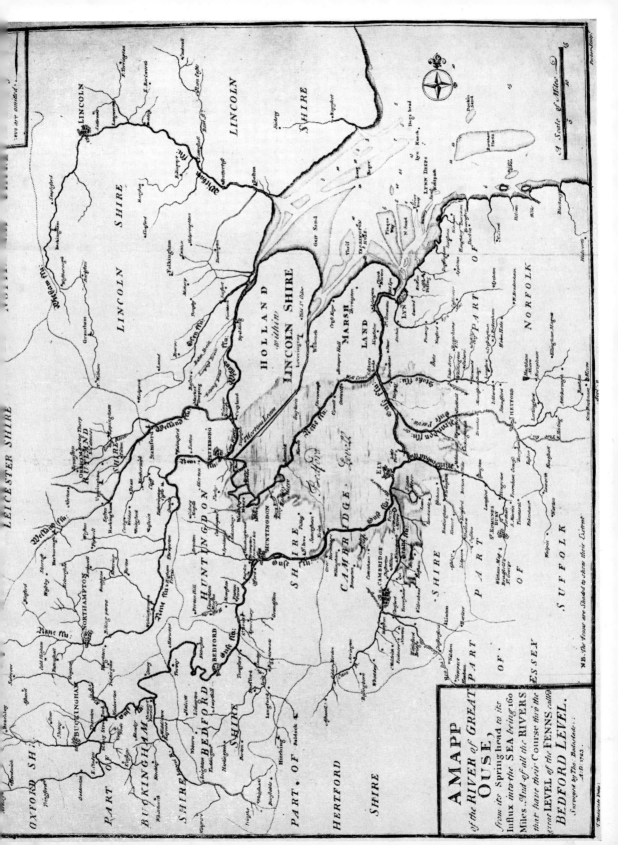

A MAPP

of the RIVER of GREAT

OUSE,

from its Spring head to its
Influx into the SEA being 160
Miles. And of all the RIVERS
that have their Course thro the
great LEVEL of the FENNS, called
BEDFORD LEVEL.

Surveyd by Tho: Badeslade:
A:D: 1725

N.B. The Seaes are Shaded to Shew their Extent

A Scale of Miles

went about things. He, on the other hand, was anxious to avoid a situation in which he would be subjected to meddling by enthusiastic amateurs whose main motive was to ensure that their money was made to go as far as possible.

The talks continued over a long period of time during which the Adventurers' financial position became more and more difficult but eventually agreement was reached with Vermuyden on 25th January, 1649. Under the terms of the agreement Vermuyden was still subject to a certain amount of control and there was a limit of £100,000 placed upon the total amount of work to be carried out. In fact it is difficult to understand just what all the wrangling was about when one realises that in the end Vermuyden relinquished much of that for which he had argued.

Work in the Fens went ahead, again not without difficulty, and to all intents and purposes the scheme was complete in 1652.

The principles of the drainage system which Vermuyden introduced are relatively easy to follow. He saw that the immense waterload on a large section of the river Ouse could be lessened if he cut new channels from Earith 20 miles or so north to Denver. These two channels are open to tidal water and it was argued that the movement of the tides would help to scour the seaward junction and keep it clear for outflowing waters. Also

The Old Bedford River, Earith. One of Vermuyden's drainage cuts for The Bedford Adventurers.

R. Tibbs

Doorway, Vermuyden's House   *Cambridge News*

the division of the tides into two streams would lessen the necessary height of the retaining banks and render much bank work in the Ouse unnecessary. The space between the two drains is, as I have indicated in an earlier chapter, "wash" land to cope with times of high flood. Denver Sluice at the junction of these two cuts and the old Ouse was built to regulate the out-flow of the Ouse at this point.

Vermuyden also proposed a channel skirting off round the edge of the Fens to the east and cutting across the Wissey, the Little Ouse and the Lark. His idea was that this would intercept flood waters coming down these rivers from parts of Suffolk and Norfolk and provide it with an alternative route to Denver. Again the load would be taken off the original course of the Ouse through Ely and Littleport.

In fact this channel was never built by Vermuyden but the Great Ouse River Board in recent years planned a scheme which worked on a similar principle and this has now been completed. It was known that there were deficiencies in the flood protection schemes of the area just after World War II but a shortage of men and materials hampered the work. Fears about the safety of the Fenland were realised in the great flood of 1947. This was the greatest flood of which there is any record and a total of 37,000 acres of Fenland lay underwater. Banks were breached in many places and as a result a new and enlarged scheme was immediately prepared. It was this scheme which followed so closely the course originally proposed by Vermuyden.

The modern channel is known as the Cut Off channel, and runs from the river Lark at Barton Mills to Denver Sluice, a distance of twenty seven and a half miles. It travels round the outer edge of the Fens and is carried in concrete syphons when it passes underneath the Lark, the Wissey and the Little Ouse. Connections are provided at the junctions with the rivers to enable the full flow or part of the flow of the streams to be diverted into the Cut Off channel. Construction of the channel was a major undertaking and involved the construction of 20 road bridges, 12 accommodation bridges (those connecting, say, one part of a farm to another), and three railway bridges.

Further north the scheme also included the construction of the Relief Channel which runs from Denver to the outskirts of Kings Lynn. This channel can carry a flood five per cent greater than that of 1947. The entire flood protection scheme was completed in September 1964 at a total cost of £10,452,000 of which the government contributed a 90 per cent grant. Mr. W. E. Doran, who was Chief Engineer to the Great Ouse River Board, as it was then called, pointed out that the value of the food produced in the Fens amounted to over £20 million a year and on that basis alone the cost of protection had not been excessive.

The remainder of the Fen drainage is achieved by 73 Internal Drainage Districts. Modern drainage practice provides for a pumping capacity of 20 to 25 tons of water a minute per thousand acres and this has been achieved by the installation of new pumping stations including some electrically operated ones. These have the advantage that they can operate during off peak hours at low costs and can be left to run unattended during the night. They can be arranged to be self-switching when water levels reach a pre-determined point. The ideal combination therefore is a diesel driven pump for use during the day and an electric one for night use. Hitherto many pumping stations were shut down during the night because of manning difficulties—a difficulty electricity usefully solves.

It can be argued that it was the difficulties of the war years which were indirectly responsible for the inadequacies in the flood prevention system when disaster came to the Fens in 1947, but the war did bring one huge benefit. In order to improve on methods of handling and transporting the immense quantities of food grown in the Fens during those difficult years many hundreds of miles of excellent concrete roads were laid down by the government. These roads criss-cross the Fenlands area today and provide comfortable but careful motoring where once carts had to be dragged through sticky mud.

Chapter Nine

Cambridge News

ANGLERS traditionally seek peaceful surroundings, a variable stream against which to pit their wits and plenty of good sport and there is no doubt that the Great Ouse and its tributaries can offer all this and more. Apart from periods when heavy rain water or melting snow rushes down from the Buckinghamshire end of the river the Great Ouse is mainly a slow-running stream which offers some of the best coarse fishing in the country.

Tactics will obviously vary to the taste of the individual but in general ledgering will provide a good starting point both in the flood relief channel near Kings Lynn and in the deeper sections of the main river. The swing tip method of fishing, in which the top joint of the rod contains a flexible link for greater sensitivity in detecting a bite, has become increasingly popular in recent years and exponents of this technique are usually to be found in the many fishing matches which take place throughout the region.

Maggot, red worm and bread, (flake or paste) are usually the most successful baits in Ouse waters. Stewed wheat often attracts nice roach and members of the Cambridge Specimen Hunters Group who have carried out experiments with a variety of baits have had good carp on fat bacon. Hempseed, a popular bait in some districts, is barred by many angling clubs who lease waters in the Ouse area. The river contains many varieties of fish. Roach and dace predominate in the upper reaches around Buckingham but bream become more numerous the further one travels toward Bedford. From then onwards through Huntingdon and the Fenland waters to Denver anglers who are fortunate enough to find bream on the feed can usually count on excellent catches. Rudd, perch, tench and chub are common in many areas and the majority of sections contain plenty of pike. Twenty pounders are not all uncommon and a few years ago one around 38 lbs. was taken from the Old Bedford river near Welney.

Fishing above Buckingham near the source of the Ouse is difficult because many of the banks are private and strictly controlled. From Buckingham onwards the water becomes generally available to anglers who have paid their appropriate licences and club dues although there are still natural hazards for the banks are often lined with tall rushes and hidden by massed foilage. Dredging in the upper reaches has been controversial but the fact remains that it has speeded up the flow of the stream to some extent, and the increased oxygenation plus restocking by the Great Ouse River Authority has resulted in some excellent fishing.

Some of the best sport is to be had when the early frosts have removed some of the weeds immediately after weed cutting in September. This part of the river is famous for its chub fishing and these are usually to be found in deeper holes towards the centre of the stream where the current has reduced the amount of weed. The actual catch may be easy enough but bringing the fish ashore through the weed banks may present problems.

Downstream toward Newport Pagnell bream, perch and pike are plentiful and record catches of roach and bream have often been reported. The river presents some very attractive stretches for the angler who is appreciative of the countryside as well as his sport and the winding character of the stream will give him much to think about when deciding which spot to fish. The Newport Pagnell water extends from Gayhurst Cottages downstream to the Cutthroat Spinney, a distance of about two and a half miles, and here there are most species with some excellent small pike to liven things up a bit. There is also good fishing just below the Olney Road bridge and Sharnbrook village record quantities of bream have fallen to experienced anglers who not only realised that they had run into a shoal of fish, but who knew how to make the best of it.

Shoaling is a characteristic of Ouse fishing which can crop up at unlikely times and produce curious results. It is often found in the Flood Relief Channel which, although basically part of the flood protection scheme, now offers excellent fishing. Anyone who finds himself fishing a shoal can have magnificent sport, whilst an angler a short distance

Fishing on the Cam at Horningsea—*Cambridge News*

A Fenland bridge across the Little Ouse

away may have a hopeless day. This was well demonstrated in 1967 when the championship of the National Federation of Anglers was fished in the Relief Channel. The winner, Eddie Townsin, a member of the Cambridge Fish Preservation and Angling Society, caught well over 40 lbs of fish, mainly bream. Most of the other 1,100 competitors found little or nothing and this was not due to inexperience, for they included many of the country's finest anglers.

Once below Eynesbury the Ouse begins to widen. Gone are the high rushes and narrow runs of the upper river, and bream, chub, roach and dace provide good sport. Through St. Neots and down to Brampton and Huntingdon the chub are particularly fine. A seven pound three ounce specimen was pulled from the water in this area not many years back and six pounders are always a possibility for the man with luck and skill on his side.

There is little change in the overall character of the fishing until one gets down stream beyond Earith. The water is tidal up to Brownshill Staunch and here there are bream, tench, roach and pike. Sea trout are often encountered in this section of the river. Non-migratory trout are now to be found in many parts of the Ouse and particularly in its tributaries but in many cases the fishing rights are privately owned. Grafham Water offers superb trout fishing and stocks are continually being built up.

A good catch taken near Denver—Cambridge News

Vermuyden's cuts, the Old Bedford River and New Bedford River or Hundred Foot Drain offer good fishing particularly with bream and pike. They also contain pike-perch, otherwise known as zander, and it was from this section that the biggest pike-perch ever caught in Britain — 11¾ lbs — was landed in 1934. Cambridge University Department of Zoology confirmed the fish as a pike-perch and it was subsequently mounted in the traditional glass case.

The Old West River, the original course of the Great Ouse until Vermuyden made his cuts north to Denver, can offer some excellent fishing. It runs from Earith past Haddenham through to the Cam at the Fish and Duck corner where the Ouse regains its identity and is winding and weedy in character. The meadows on either side are green and quiet and at Stretham and Twentypence there are still some splendid hedgerows which, on a blustery day, make good wind breaks. There are some fine fish in the Old West, mainly bream, tench, rudd and pike. Roach are also plentiful although mainly small. The stream tends to be rather sluggish and overgrown in summer although, as one would expect, it improves from September onwards. Where the Old West joins the Cam the water is both wide and deep and from Adelaide Bridge down to Littleport ledgering is the most successful technique especially when used with a swing tip rod or some other form of bite indicator system. Shallow swims close to the bank often favour roach, but generally the accent is on bream.

Towards Kings Lynn both the main river and the flood channel provide good fishing and are "big" waters in every sense of the word. Ledgering remains the method to use and the river holds all species of fish with bream predominating. Below Kings Lynn the water is often salty and the angler runs into flounders and eels. But bream are to be found and sea trout often make a day's fishing worth while.

The tributaries of the Ouse largely consist of private trout fishing at their upper ends but in many cases excellent coarse fishing is available in the lower reaches. Among the largest is the Cam which offers some good fishing controlled by a number of different clubs and societies. Good roach, dace and bream are often available. Two other tributaries which have some useful water available to the angler are the Ivel, which flows into the Ouse above Tempsford Bridge in Bedfordshire, and the Ousel which joins the main river at Newport Pagnell. Of eastern tributaries of the Ouse the Wissey, which reaches the main stream below Hilgay, produces some of the finest fishing. This very pleasant little river has some of the characteristics of a south country chalk stream and holds some superb fish, chub in particular.

We have talked in this chapter about all the well known and relatively common types of fish which provide the anglers of the Ouse and its associated rivers with so much good sport. But there is one fish, now very rare in Britain which, it is believed can still be found in the Ouse. This is the Burbot and it is now the subject of an intensive search by the British Ichthyological Society.

In Britain burbot have only been found east of a line from Durham down through Lincolnshire and just touching the Wash. There is no doubt that it was once a good deal more common than it is now although it is doubtful whether it has ever been plentiful. Today it is the country's rarest freshwater fish and so little is known about it by anglers that few would be able to identify it if they caught one. The burbot is a scavenger and a predator and prefers cold dark deepish water. It is nocturnal and only feeds at night and for this reason is unlikely to be taken by the angler who keeps normal hours. Since the turn of the century only about 30 burbot have been recorded in this country. Those from the Ouse were taken by night anglers and eel fishers before interest in the fish reached its present level.

The Ichthyological Society know of one caught by a lad near Wilton Bridge who returned it to the water; they are aware of a more recent capture near the sluice at Hockwold when a Feltwell eel fisher pulled one out weighing about one and a half pounds. Before the burbot hunters got to him it had been eaten by the cat! Since then,

Cruisers on the Old West showing excellent manners in keeping their speed down   *M. Manni*

and with the permission of the Great Ouse River Authority, the Society have instituted full scale hunts for the fish using frogmen, traps, two-way radio and many other modern scientific aids, but the burbot remains elusive.

About eighteen inches long when fully grown burbot have been known to reach a weight of about nine pounds. They are mottled brown in colour, although this does vary according to the locality, and have a broad head and very large mouth. Like its close relative the cod, it has a single barbule beneath the chin and there are two very small barbules hardly visible behind the nostrils.

Because of its rarity in Britain and of its great age as a species the burbot is a very interesting fish which may exist now if at all, only in the Great Ouse and its tributaries. Anglers on the river expect and get first class sport from what we might call everyday fish but the fact that there is a real scientific trophy to be landed gives sport in the area added appeal. Describing the one that got away is a traditional angling occupation but Ouse anglers will learn to be doubly careful, the fish they describe in the bar could be burbot — a trophy indeed.

Fishing near Adelaide

Chapter Ten

Headquarters of The Great Ouse River Authority, Cambridge   *R. Tibbs*

THE entire length of the river Great Ouse, its tributaries and the water resources of the area through which it flows, are controlled by the Great Ouse River Authority, one of the largest authorities of its type in the country. It came into existence on 15th October 1964 but it was not until 1st April of the following year that it took up its full responsibilities for the area which had previously been administered by the Great Ouse River Board. The essential difference between the old Board and the new Authority is an almost complete reversal of policy. The former had been primarily concerned with the disposal of water, its drainage and subsequent conveyance to the sea. When the new River Authority came into being it took on the responsibility for water conservation as well.

It was thus that in a short time those who had for years concerned themselves with draining the waters of the Great Ouse away from the land now found themselves thinking about the conservation of the water and its ultimate supply to public, commercial and domestic use. The Great Ouse River Authority is now housed in magnificent new headquarters in Cambridge; in addition to normal office accommodation it is fully equipped with laboratories, drawing offices, and a technical library. The building which is five storeys high, and has a floor area of 32,515 square feet, cost £184,665. Various Government Ministries appoint a number of members to the Boards and these include representatives of local authorities, industry as well as private individuals. There are also members who represent landowners subject to a drainage charge and various types of industry. Together they form a number of working committees and a glance at the titles of some of these gives an excellent idea of the work carried out; they cover flood protection, land drainage, general purposes, finance and estates, water resources, fisheries and pollution prevention.

Heading the large staff are the principal officers, the Clerk, the Chief Engineer, the Treasurer, the Chief Pollution Prevention Officer and the Fisheries Officer. Under its responsibility for all general water resources in the area the board controls and issues all licences without which no water can be abstracted from the area. This means that anybody pumping water from a river or pumping it from an artesian well must hold an abstraction licence issued by the Board. This applies to the smallest smallholder and the biggest water company alike and the issuing of licences and the calculation of available water reserves form a very large part of the work.

Denver Sluice   *Lynn News and Advertiser*

Brownshill Staunch near St. Ives   *M. Manni*

The Great Ouse River Authority is one of the very few in the south east of the country which has a positive surplus of water and plans are already in existence for supplying the Essex River Authority with water for its rivers. This is by an underground pipe connecting the Ouse with the Stour. This in turn would be used to feed two large public reservoirs and thereby increase supplies to an area not quite so fortunate as that of the Great Ouse. Naturally there is resistance to the idea in some quarters, probably based on a fear that one day the Great Ouse area will not have enough for itself coupled with the tradition that what falls on one man's land is his own property.

An extensive raingauge network covers the region and this in conjunction with modern equipment for measuring river flow gives the Authority a very good idea, at any one point, of the amount of water which has fallen and the extent to which it has reached the rivers.

Man of the Fens

Cambridge News

Drainage continues to represent much of the Authority's day to day work although it is now convinced that the danger of serious flood in the Fens is over as far as anyone can see into the foreseeable future. This means that no longer will the fenman have to fear the sort of catastrophic floods which occurred in 1947, the worst in the history of the Fens. An exceptionally high tide backed by mountainous waves whipped up by hurricane force winds conspired to breach and then partly destroy the flood banks in many places. By the end of March 1947 37,000 acres of Fenland lay under water and it was obvious that a new and enlarged scheme for flood protection ought to be prepared. By June the Fens had been pumped dry and in December the banks were ready for the next onslaught. March 1948 passed without incident and for a while the Fens were safe. The next serious flood occurred on the night of 31st January 1953 when an exceptionally high tide in the North sea broke defences in both England and Holland. It showed up weaknesses in the revised scheme which resulted in the present system of defences — a system which makes the Fens as safe as they have ever been.

But all this requires constant maintenance and renewal and day-to-day work of the Great Ouse River Authority covers the cutting of grass, disposal of rubbish on embankments, the structural and mechanical maintenance of locks, sluices, weirs and

Old methods are often still best so a man and his scythe set off to work on the river's banks

Cambridge News

Baits Bite lock — the first downstream from Cambridge *M. Manni*

pumping stations, river regulation, weed cutting and channel cleaning, vermin destruction, fencing, surveys and bank patrols. The Authority has extensive workshops at Ely which are able to carry out the manufacture of new steel parts for locks and sluices. They cover over five acres and the various processes which can be carried out include shot-blasting, metal spraying, arc, oxy-acetylene and spot welding, gear cutting, hobbing and surface grinding, turning, milling and shaping, shearing, rolling, punching, drilling and riveting. With these workshops the Authority can make all necessary repairs including complete overhauls of its plant which ranges from 100 c.c. power saws, which sound like angry wasps when in use, to 500 b.h.p. stationary diesel engines driving twin 45 inch pumping units. The workshops also have two slipways, one equipped with power capstans, and capable of receiving for repair tugs, barges and floating dredgers up to 150 tons displacements.

The Authority's fisheries officer keeps an expert eye on the welfare and stocks of fish throughout the Great Ouse Region and supervises a continuous programme of restocking. The Authority has its own trout hatchery at Snailwell and is able to produce supplies of trout in large numbers, but the huge demand for these fish, particularly when stocking Grafham Water, has also meant that large additional quantities of fish had to be bought from commercial trout hatcheries. Not so long ago herons provided the staff of the Snailwell hatchery with problems by persistently killing or maiming trout of all sizes. Both shooting and trip wires failed to stop them and eventually nylon netting was used very effectively to cover the breeding ponds.

The Authority's pollution officer and his staff keep a continuous check on the quality of water throughout the region and any reports of pollution are investigated immediately. This is work which requires continuous vigilance and one which relies to a large extent on public co-operation both in avoiding pollution and in reporting it as soon as it occurs.

All this work may have its serious aspects but to me it is reassuring to find that the recreational aspect of the Ouse rivers is not overlooked by its governing authority. The continued maintenance of the waterways to allow the navigation of pleasure boats is all part of the task and in places where the Authority does not have its own lock keeper living locally special keys are supplied on hire.

It might be helpful to recall at this point the limits of navigation for boats. Along the Bedford section of the Ouse the limit occurs at Tempsford. In the Ely Ouse one can navigate the Wissey to Stoke Ferry, the Little Ouse to Brandon, the Lark to Jude's Ferry, West Row, Suffolk, the Burwell Lode to Burwell and the Cam up to Cambridge. Boats travelling along the Old West pass through Hermitage lock from which they can cruise up to Tempsford. Strangers fail to realise that there is a short length of river with two locks in it at Bedford which is available for cruising but at the moment it is cut off from the main section of Ouse navigation. There is also a connection available between the waters of the Ouse and the many drains and streams which lie between Ely and Peterborough and which are known as the Middle Level. It is thus that the trip can be made from the Ouse to the waters of the River Nene which has its estuary to the west of the Ouse in the Wash.

This connection is maintained by the Great Ouse Authority at Welches Dam which is about half way down the Old Bedford River. I always think that a less boring way of getting into the Middle Level by water is through Salter's Lode which connects to the main river through a lock just below Denver. This point is just above the limit for hire

Hermitage Lock which has now been modernised   *D. Monk*

boats so it is quite "legal" for the holidaymaker. It travels across to the oddly named Pophams Eau and avoids the long cruise down the ruler straight Old Bedford river. The Great Ouse Authority tells me that it is possible to take a boat through to the River Nene and thence via Northampton through to the Grand Union Canal.

Thus the water system connects through to the Midlands and the Ouse administrators can fairly claim to bridge the gap between the industrial centre of England and the tranquil waters of Norfolk, Suffolk and Essex. Without such constant attention the waterways would rapidly degenerate to the weedy mess that Vermuyden and many others before him tackled in one way or another. Perhaps the finest tribute one can pay is to point out the quiet and wonderfully efficient way in which this organisation carries out its many tasks. So quietly in fact that the average man in the street is more or less totally unaware that the Authority exists. A vast multitude of people, including farmers, landowners, housewives, sportsmen and holidaymakers, owe a considerable debt of gratitude to the vision and skill of the Bedford Level Adventurers under Vermuyden and the generations of others who have followed and continued the magnificent work of harnessing the river to the needs of man.

Chapter Eleven

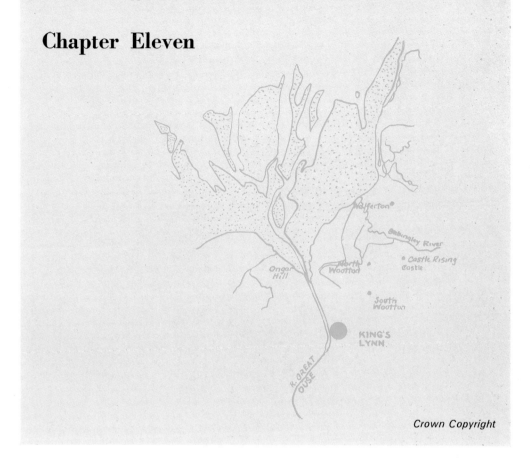

Crown Copyright

THE final stretch of the Ouse, that from Littleport to the sea, is full of excitement and interest. What other river can claim a story to feed the imagination to match that of King John's lost treasure? Even here the Ouse springs a surprise for the Ouse in which King John lost so much, including many retainers, is no longer the Ouse we know today. Some time after the unfortunate King's adventure, the river's course was changed and where once it flowed through Wisbech it now flows through Kings Lynn.

It was in 1216 that the King made his fateful journey from Kings Lynn to Wisbech and a chronicler of the time, Matthew Paris, gives us the most accurate description of what took place. It is from his remarks that subsequent treasure hunters have started their quest, so far without success. Paris wrote in Latin, but translated he said, "Leaving the town of Lynn, which he (the King) had greatly distinguished and honoured with donations he attempted to force a passage over the water which is called the Welle stream, and there suddenly and irrecoverably lost all his waggons, treasures, costly

The Boat Haven, Littleport

M. Manni

goods and regalia. A whirlpool in the middle of the water absorbed all into its depths, with men and horses, so that hardly one escaped to announce the misfortune to the King".

At the time the Ouse and the Nene joined forces just outside Wisbech and flowed through the town as one joint river, commonly accepted as being the "Welle Stream" Paris wrote about. But efforts to improve drainage at a very early date resulted in a serious mistake and one which was to reduce the importance of Wisbech as a port. Sometime between 1215 and 1270 a leam or dyke two miles long was cut from the Great Ouse at Littleport. The bulk of the Great Ouse water then carved its way out to sea through the Little Ouse Estuary while the Nene, left to wander through Wisbech on its own, did not have enough force to keep the huge inland estuary of the time free from silt.

In addition, the inability of the water to escape easily at Wisbech resulted in it backing up on itself and adding to the flooded areas in the neighbourhood. At Lynn the extra load of water was also proving too much for existing banks and flooding was occurring as well. Attempts were made to divert the water back onto its original course, but the slit in the Wisbech estuary and the weight of water at the newly cut leam proved too much and the Ouse has remained in its changed course from that day to this.

The annual big boats race soon after the start at Littleport bridge   *Ely Standard*

Watson in his "History of Wisbech" tells us that at the time the haven of Lynn was only about six poles wide and served to discharge water coming down from the Little Ouse or Brandon River, and the small rivers of Stoke, Setch and Nar. It is a much wider and more comprehensive port today.

It is possible to judge the route King John took from Lynn to Wisbech with some accuracy and although it is popularly believed that he lost his men and treasure in the Wash, it is quite clear that the mishap occurred in or very close to Wisbech which to-day is nineteen miles inland. John left Lynn on 11th October 1216 and it seems likely that he crossed the Little Ouse (now the Great Ouse) near Wiggenhall St. Germans, and then followed high ground by Wiggenhall St. Marys, Lord's Bridge, and Tilney Buck to Tilney St. Lawrence. He would then probably have made his way to Walsoken travelling along high ground which has been called "The Highways". From there it seemed likely that he would attempt the crossing to Wisbech at a point where the river was fairly narrow and it therefore follows that the treasure, if it exists, lies somewhere on a line roughly drawn between Walsoken and Wisbech.

If John crossed at any point nearer the Wash he would have found himself faced with water a mile to a mile-and-a-half in width and headstrong though he was it is difficult to believe he would have attempted this. It is pleasant to think of his treasure buried in the mud somewhere in this few square miles of Wisbech suburb. One day highly sensitive scientific instruments may even yet smell it out.

It is no reflection upon present Wisbech to say that one does not have to delve far into its past to find fairly primitive surroundings. The streets were not paved until 1810. Until then wooden planks were placed across the streets in bad weather to enable pedestrians to cross without getting themselves too muddy. At night the streets were in semi-darkness and the only illumination available was by lamps lit by whale oil. One does not need to go back much further, to the 1790's for example, to find press gangs roaming the streets on the lookout for any able bodied man who would be carried off to serve in the navy, often without even opportunity to bid farewell to his family.

I have indicated elsewhere in this book that the Fenman is a cautious type not given to rushing into things. Vermuyden grew to know this dislike of change and of 'foreigners' and I think that no story indicates this traditional stoicism so well as that which relates to the heyday of the fast stage coach services. In due course Wisbech was connected to London with a through route which was good for these days but there were those in the town who actively campaigned against such a link with the capital. It was felt that it would become a temptation to ladies and gentlemen "to spend their money in extravagance and pleasure".

The coming of the railways and the opportunity they gave to move goods around the country with much greater freedom had an adverse effect on Wisbech as a port. In 1847 cargo through the dock amounted to 167,443 tons but eight years later this figure

The Custom House, Kings Lynn

Lynn News and Advertiser

Part of Kings Lynn Docks

Lynn News and Advertiser

was down by about half. Anyone interested in the history of the region should visit Wisbech museum. All visitors agree that it is far more comprehensive and interesting than anyone would imagine from a casual glance at the exterior.

Kings Lynn sits astride the Great Ouse at the point where it enters the sea. For the great majority of East Anglians it is the place one passes through on the way to Hunstanton but to ignore Lynn is to overlook an ancient port of immense charm. Lynn was a port in Norman times and centuries later in the mid-nineteenth century was busily exporting corn at a time when home prices were fixed by the Corn Laws. Its chief import trade used to be coal from Newcastle which was brought round the coast in specially constructed barges. The famous Stourbridge Fair at Cambridge received most of its goods by water from the port of Lynn and many is the time that the Borough of Cambridge has petitioned Parliament about poor navigational prospects between itself and the old Norfolk port.

In spite of its venerable age Kings Lynn remains one of East Anglia's most active ports. As congestion and delays have built up in the docks of the Port of London Midland industrialists have favoured Lynn in a search for other outlets for exports to the Continent. Exports through Lynn have risen and there is no doubt that it makes a significant contribution to the country's economy. New industries have gone to Lynn and it now has maltings, breweries, corn mills, canning factories, a sugar factory and many other assets in addition to those which one would associate with a busy port.

The town is not without its old buildings. Until recent years all road traffic on its way up to Hunstanton and the Norfolk seaside resorts beyond had to pass under the old fifteenth century South Gate. Now a fine new by-pass relieves much of the traffic load on the old town, a development for which both residents and motorists are most grateful. There are many splendid houses of the Georgian period and earlier, and a particularly quaint yet charming building is the Custom House designed in 1683 by Henry Bell, a local architect. It was here that George Vancouver (1758-1795) worked for a time. This famous navigator and explorer of the western coast of North America gave his name of the famous city and seaport in British Columbia.

From Lynn one can see the point at which the Great Ouse empties itself in the Wash, a hundred and sixty miles or so from its starting point near Brackley. With most rivers this would represent the end of the story, but not so with the Great Ouse. As we have seen it is capable of producing many surprises, its change of route from Wisbech to Kings Lynn, and the fact that it changes its name about half way along its course to become the Old West River. There is now a possibility that Ouse waters will not lose their identity after leaving Lynn and that they will flow on to fill one of the largest man-made fresh water reservoirs in the country. A desk study is being carried out into the possibility of a barrage or huge dam across part of the Wash. This would trap fresh water leaving the mouth of the Ouse and retain it for future use. A tentative suggestion published at various times has put the huge retaining wall somewhere in the region of Heacham village near Hunstanton. From there it might run at right angles to the coast out into the Wash only to turn through ninety degrees to reach the coast again somewhere near the mouth of the Nene.

The difficulties surrounding such a scheme would be enormous and the cost equally great. Sea locks would have to be incorporated in the wall in order that shipping might still reach Lynn. The control of outgoing water against the levels of the tide would also present headaches and the ecological changes that such a large expanse of fresh water would provide in the countryside around it would also have to be considered. But against this it would make an immense contribution to one of the most aggravating problems of the future, the supply of sufficient quantities of fresh water, and it would also enable a coast road to run round the top of the wall and make the journey from Boston to Hunstanton appreciably shorter.

If the scheme does prove a possibility, and those masters of hydrological problems, the Dutch, have offered assistance, there remains the cost. The capital required for such an undertaking would be considerable and future governments would obviously weigh the advantages and disadvantages most carefully before committing themselves to such a far-reaching proposal. But it would not be the first time the Great Ouse has been the subject of farsightedness, of great vision and of great cost. It is no newcomer to controversy and it is thoroughly familiar with bitter argument. But it has brought enormous benefits to the entire country and it may as yet do so again.

Waterside scene, Kings Lynn *Lynn News and Advertiser*

Appendix One

GREAT OUSE BOATBUILDERS AND OPERATORS ASSOCIATION

Members of the Association are always pleased to help anyone wanting to hire craft on the river or who wish to admire it from the shore.

All boatyards provide hire craft and most offer facilities for petrol and diesel fuel, fresh water, waste disposal and replacement ice packs for insulated cold boxes. They are as follows:—

Cambridge   H. C. Banham Ltd. Telephone: Cambridge 53093

Earith   *Hermitage Boatyard. Telephone: Earith 555

             F. W. Carrington. Telephone: Earith 400

Ely   *Appleyard and Lincoln & Co. Ltd. Telephone: Ely 2244

Huntingdon   *Elysian Holidays Ltd. Telephone: Huntingdon 3060

Offord   Buckden Marina. Telephone: Buckden 355

St. Ives   L. H. Jones. Telephone: St. Ives 3463

St. Neots   White House Boatyard. Telephone: St. Neots 2763

*Elysian Holidays Ltd. hire craft available at these yards.

The following local associations could be of interest:— Cam Sailing Club; Cambridge Motor Boat Club; Denver Sailing Club; East Anglian Waterways Association; Ely Sailing Club; Great Ouse Boating Association and The Ouse Valley River Club.

This above lists and that of hotels and licenced houses on the following page were provided by the Great Ouse Boatbuilders & Operators Association. They have advised that they should be used as a guide only since they are by no means a comprehensive list of available facilities and amenities.

RIVERSIDE HOTELS AND LICENCED HOUSES

as provided by Great Ouse Boatbuilders and Operators Association

The following riverside hotels and licenced houses can usually provide services as indicated. Visitors are, however, advised to check with the establishments since people and circumstances change and facilities may be added to or subtracted from at any time.

Place	Establishment	M	W	R	D	I
Brandon Creek	The Ship	M	W	R	D	I
Clayhithe	Bridge Restaurant	M	W	R	D	—
Downham Market	Jenyns Arms, Denver Sluice	M	—	R	D	—
Earith	Crown Inn	M	W	R	—	—
Ely	Cutter Inn	M	W	—	D	—
Fen Ditton	Plough Inn	M	W	R	D	—
Godmanchester	Royal Oak	—	—	—	—	—
Holywell	Ye Olde Ferry Boat Inn	M	W	—	D	—
Littleport	Black Horse, Sandhill Bridge	M	W	R	D	—
Little Thetford	Fish and Duck Inn	M	W	R	D	—
Prickwillow	Waggon and Horses	M	W	R	D	—
St. Ives	Pike and Eel, Overcote Ferry	M	W	R	—	—
	Dolphin Inn	M	W	R	—	—
St. Neots	White House Club and Restaurant	M	W	R	—	I
	Bridge Hotel	M	W	—	D	—
Southery	Ferry Boat	M	W	R	—	—
Stoke Ferry	The Bull	M	W	R	D	—
Stretham Bridge	Royal Oak	M	W	R	—	—
Tempsford	Anchor Hotel	M	W	R	D	—
Ten Mile Bank	The Windmill	—	W	R	—	—
West Row	Judes Ferry Inn	M	W	R	D	—
Wyton (**Hunts**)	Three Jolly Butchers	M	W	R	—	—

Key. **M** — Moorings   **R** — Waste Disposal
W — Fresh Water   **D** — Dining
I — Ice Pack Replacement

In addition to other things ice pack replacements are available at C. W. Brown's Stores, **Hilgay** and the Post Office and General stores at **Prickwillow.**

Appendix 2

The diagrammatic map shows the distances between various points on the river.

H. C. Banham Ltd. of Cambridge provide an excellent map of the navigable waters which includes links with the River Nene. The One-Inch and Quarter-Inch Ordnance Maps are also very helpful. Local newspapers provide a wealth of information about the area. Early closing days vary considerably and it is advisable, especially on holiday afloat, to check on those in the areas in which you intend to cruise.

I cannot stress too strongly that the future of the waterways of the Great Ouse lies in our hands. There are a few "Dos & Don'ts" which will help to ensure maximum enjoyment for all using the river. They will also help those who maintain it.

DO keep speed down when afloat to prevent damage to river banks, other craft and riverside property.

DO slow when passing anglers and keep well clear of their lines.

DO ask for help when you need it and be ready to help others.

DO ensure, when afloat, that children and adults unable to swim have and wear life jackets.

DO keep the volume of your radio set down and show respect and courtesy to all others.

DON'T leave litter on the banks or throw it in the water

DON'T damage trees or fences nor leave field gates open.

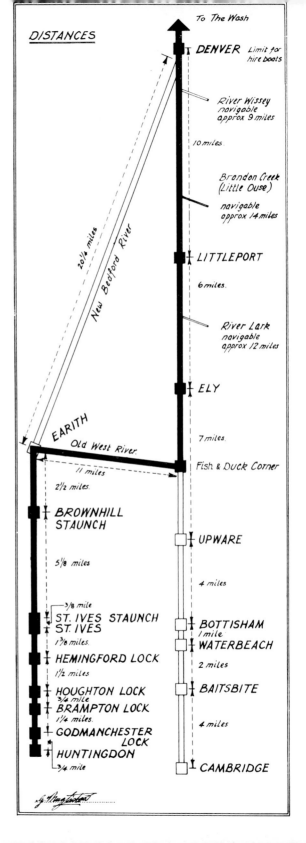

INDEX

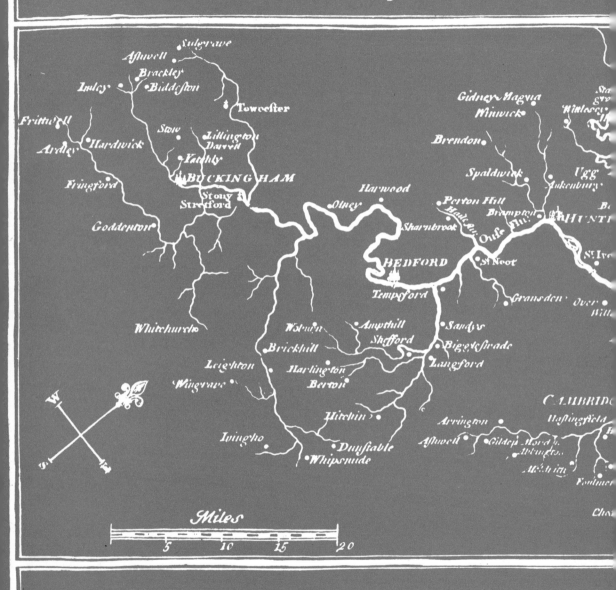

A SURVEY of the OUSE from i

to its Influx into the SEA b

Taken from T. Badeslade's History of the Navigation of the Port of King's Lynn 1